ENCOUNTERING GOD
IN THE ABYSS

The Fiery Arrow Collection

Editors: Hein Blommestijn and Jos Huls of Titus Brandsma Institute

Advisory Board:

The *Fiery Arrow series* aims at the publication of books which connect their readers with the legacy of great teachers of spirituality from the distant and more recent past. Readers are offered a language and conceptual framework which can lead them to a deepened understanding of the spiritual life. The treasures of the spiritual tradition form a veritable "school of love", which is accessible to all who in contemplation desire to be touched by the fire of divine love. In 1270 A.D. Nicholas of France, former prior general of the Carmelites, wrote a letter bearing the title *Fiery Arrow* to his fellow brothers to urge them to call to mind again the fire of the beginning in which, in silence and solitude, they were consumed by the inescapable claim of the One. Based on the Carmelite tradition, this series seeks to share this spiritual legacy – which presents itself in a multiplicity of cultures and traditions – with all those who in a great variety of ways are in search of interior life and the fire of love. The series, which is grounded in scientific research, is aimed at a broad public interested in spirituality.

The Titus Brandsma Institute is an academic center of research in spirituality founded in 1968 by the Catholic University of Nijmegen and the Carmelite Order. Titus Brandsma, who from 1923 on was a professor of philosophy and the history of mysticism, especially that of the Low Countries, died in 1942 as a martyr in the Nazi death camp of Dachau and was beatified in 1985. The Institute continues his research in spirituality and mysticism with a staff of assistants and in collaboration with other researchers. In addition to this and other series, the Institute publishes the international periodical *Studies in Spirituality* and the series *Studies in Spirituality Supplement* (Peeters, Louvain).

Already published in this series:

ENCOUNTERING GOD IN THE ABYSS

Titus Brandsma's Spiritual
Journey

by
CONSTANT DÖLLE

Translated by
JOHN VRIEND

PEETERS
LEUVEN – PARIS – DUDLEY, MA
2002

ISBN 90-429-1163-8
D. 2002/0602/84

Table of Contents

Introduction

A man in dark clothing and wearing a handsome black hat rang the doorbell of a house in the *Oranjestraat* on the east side of Winschoten. Small and energetic, he moved along in rapid steps. The street was quiet and dull; the houses were all the same – duplexes under a single roof surrounded by a garden. The year was 1923. As examiner for the final exams of secondary schools, Titus Brandsma had come to Winschoten in Groningen, and stayed at the rectory. The priest, listing the names of the neighbors, had probably said to him: "the Dölle family is also from Friesland." So he dropped by simply to chat as Frisians among themselves. Up until 1924, Etty Hillesum, two years older than the author of this book, lived next door. She was then nine years old. Next to the Hillesums lived Constant Dölle's piano teacher. The children played on the street; it was a quiet street and at the time only one car was parked there. It is likely that Titus Brandsma and Etty Hillesum had, without knowing it, seen each other. Brandsma loved to stop by at the Dölles to talk with Constant's mother. Her mother was a DeBoer and Brandsma had a cousin, the Carmelite Casimir de Boer. They wondered if perhaps they were somehow related.

Constant Dölle, seven years old at the time, saw a simple man who inspired confidence. Someone who had an interest in the family and was good to have contact with. Looking back he said:

> He is a person you can absolutely trust. That is possible only if that person believes in God. For then he can surrender himself, let himself go, and say: 'let things happen as You want them to.' With such a person you can take your chances, because he does not give priority to his own interests. With a person like that you will never end up holding the bag.[1]

[1] In a interview about his memories on Titus Brandsma.

Titus was an unexpected role model who was ranked next to the teacher of the third grade in elementary school, Mr. Altepost. "If you want to become a genuine person, you have to become like that man."

Later as a student at the gymnasium in Zenderen, Constant heard a school supervisor say: "Titus Brandsma is in the building." This was said in a low voice and with much respect. This struck him, because he did not know that Brandsma was now a professor and a special person. During his theological studies in Merkelbeek he saw him several times. Titus frequently came there because he was a close friend of Hubert Driessen. Their last encounter occurred in that period:

> I last met Titus Brandsma shortly before he was taken prisoner, i.e., early in January 1942. It was getting dark and we sat down to dinner. A strange and uncertain mood hung in the air. The country was awash in dangers. What would happen to people who had openly joined the resistance? We could not think of any reassuring words to say. The feeling of powerlessness produced a mood of resignation. We stayed at the table longer than usual. Titus was scheduled to leave shortly afterward.
>
> He walked past me, a fragile figure but forceful in his movements. For a moment he stopped and turned around as if to make sure not to forget to say goodbye to anyone. At that moment, for the last time, I saw his smile. Often, in my memory, I have seen him walk past me – with that smile. That face, in which all trace of fierceness was lacking and which conveyed a sense of indomitable assurance, has stuck with me. That smile is a part of it. At the time I thought that if he were to close his eyes and everything fell silent, and he would look at himself, his own interior world, that smile would still be there.
>
> One would like to know what he thought of himself. Perhaps he had his pride and was easily offended. But – not a word about that. He was a man trained in controlling his deepest feelings. He had no need to call attention to himself. He did not impress one as a conceited person secretly in search of recognition. That was not something he was familiar with.
>
> At the time I was astonished at that smile and, after everything I heard about him later, I was even more amazed. It was an inward-

looking smile, not overshadowed by deep anxieties over a safe life and great successes – a smile which contained the pure light within itself.

Constant Dölle was ordained to the priesthood on July 12, 1942, and celebrated his first mass on the first Sunday in August of that year. On that Sunday they learned that Titus Brandsma had died in Dachau on July 26. Although Dölle never became a Brandsma specialist, Titus did play a role throughout his entire life. Yet it is no accident that he learned to know Titus Brandsma in his youth and has now written a book about him. He himself calls this "a kind of divine dispensation by which things happen as they do."

> I marvel at the fact that I also became a Carmelite 'by accident.' In 1985 I 'accidentally' wrote my first book about Titus Brandsma. The person who had been assigned to do this for the beatification said: 'I dread this job and feel sick about the whole thing.' Then the authorities got me involved and the job had to be done in three months. Nor was it my idea to write a new book about him now. Things regularly come my way from others.

In fact, a short time after he started writing the present book, he slowly became almost completely blind. His initial reaction was that this meant the end of his project. He still hoped for a cure. When it gradually became clear that, from a medical perspective, this was no longer possible, a few people proved willing to assist him in the work of reading and writing. In that way writing Titus Brandsma's biography became a process of reconciling himself to his own situation of aging and becoming blind. In light of the experience of the end of his own possibilities, the task of describing the journey to an end which, in the case of Titus Brandsma, no longer offered any escape routes, became for him a spiritual process which yielded insight. His reply to the question what Titus Brandsma meant to him in recent years reads as follows:

> What impressed me most was his acceptance of everything that took place around him. What I learned from Titus is to accept oneself with one's own possibilities and limitations. He never talked about other possibilities: this way and no other – was the way he had to go. He opted – in freedom – to go the way he had to go. He did

this even when in the prison at Kleef he experienced a time of despair. He chose his life destiny as it was, and the circumstances in which he actually found himself as that which was completely a part of his life. There was in any case no way to escape it. Even when one must suffer pain, it is best to accept it! Titus believed in a God who arranges and orders all things. 'Acceptance' is the central word of his life. But acceptance is possible only when it is rooted in the confidence that there is a God who is committed to your well-being, even though you do not at all understand his way with you. He did not wonder what would now happen with his work and countless unfinished projects. His message, accordingly, is also very accessible for simple people: *take life as it is*. Titus saw his life's journey as the journey which was actually unfolding – and that was a dreadful one. But it was his own inasmuch as he saw it as his task, his assignment, and his calling. Reflection on the life of Titus Brandsma makes one discover the inward journey on which one finds strength and happiness because in all circumstances life is meaningful. In the extreme circumstances of his life and as a result of his relation to God Titus Brandsma became a real Carmelite, a true son of the prophet Elijah. His trust in the God who is incomprehensible was absolute, or, as he puts it: 'Sometimes God is nearby; sometimes he is far away.' Even though he found himself in jail, he knew that he was alive and that this was an incredible miracle. It was a life lived out of the conviction that everything is radically good. Titus Brandsma had to relinquish one more thing and that was his cell. This, too, he achieved.

Writing a spiritual biography is not a technical activity, even though much insight and respect is needed to deal appropriately with the source material. Authors cannot maintain a safe distance by restricting themselves to objective "facts" in an informative report. In a life story what stands out is the growing awareness of values which are central. Writers who listen to this life story carefully and respectfully record their observations. The resulting record is a reconstruction of lived experience as it unfolds in an endlessly diverse stream of events. It is a stream for which there are no ready-made words or distinctions, starting point or conclusion. It is a life that is lived from an obscure point we call "I." But it is also a life that gradually evolves as a dialogue with an even more obscure point we

gropingly call "God." We attempt, in a process of becoming
increasingly conscious and of finding the right words, to portray
the mystery of "this life" as a series of "events" and "experiences."
In search of traces of the leading figure, we sketch a history of
observations, impressions, ideas, longings, and feelings. Along these
countless lines we try to unscramble not only the mystery of this
one person but also our own face. Who really are we? How did we
become the persons we are? Is this the truth or is it a distortion aris-
ing solely from incidental impressions? How do we become the
persons we really are? How do we become the persons "God" had
in mind when he created us? Or are we our own life project? And
who will then guarantee us that this is our "truth"?

A spiritual biography attempts to lay bare the outline of the
growing awareness of God's "working" in a human life. It is the history of the struggle to accept oneself out of God's hand and hence
also the history of blockages, fears, and repressions. In many ways,
after all, we hold all sorts of things at bay in the hope of saving ourselves by the skin of our teeth: We want to understand and control, plan and organize our life. As long as we have control of our
life, we experience a sense of security. We search for a fixed point
within ourselves. We resist the "uncertainty" of the unmerited miracle of a life that we received "for nothing." But we only begin to
really live when we dare entrust ourselves to the mystery of the
creative hand of God. Having been created after God's image, our
life unfolds as an ongoing process in which we progressively grow
toward complete likeness with this image. In that way we become
the persons we essentially are. Because God sees our "beauty" we
are made beautiful. For God to see, after all, is the same as to create and to love. A spiritual biography, accordingly, describes the
growing consciousness which God's mysterious "working" brings to
light. This is the story of the indescribable miracle which occurs
in a person "in life as it is." This story introduces us readers into
the space of God's transformative "working" as this is realized also
in ourselves.

Although the story of a life is always a construction and therefore an imaginative representation, this story gives us access to the

"truth." A true biography does not relate facts and externals but the "inside story," the deep undercurrent. After all, we never possess the true life, nor can we ever retain it. Nor can it be invented or laid down in a series of deep thoughts or interesting facts. Being a mystery, a human life is "inconceivable." Although this book reflects the course of Titus Brandsma's life, it does no more than set down how he, by searching, found his way in the untrodden landscape we call his "life." On this journey the boundaries of what is conceivable and imaginable are far exceeded. With Titus Brandsma we enter an abyss of inhumanity. We, too, will have to enter it with confidence without ever abandoning our revulsion and incomprehension.

Ultimately it is not the author or "narrators" who speak to us from the platform of this book but the "readers" who in reading it become conscious of the course of their own life. This life inevitably unfolds as a journey of exploration into the same "world." At the expense of many lives and on account of the heroic courage of countless people the Nazi dictatorship was wiped out in 1945, but the horrors of inhumanity are still part of the fabric of human possibilities. By reading this book we complete and inevitably enrich it with a self-examination which belongs to our own spiritual autobiography. This book does no more than open a window on the picture of things which lie beyond what has been written. It is not Titus Brandsma who constitutes the core of this book but the journey of a person as it delineates itself as a possibility within the context of the Holocaust. Like a medieval "Life," the life of Brandsma speaks to the reader's imagination, not because a hero or a saint has been depicted but because in the portrayal of this "model" a road has been marked off for each one of us. Reading the life of this "stranger" brings us home to ourselves.

The life of Titus Brandsma is not over. He continues to live in the prayers and wordless sighs of countless people who daily visit the memorial chapel on the *Keizer Karel* square in Nijmegen and, by writing down their comments in a notebook which lies there, take him into their confidence. From him they learn to entrust themselves to God in circumstances they do not understand but which shape their journey. His intercession helps them to arrive at acceptance where, humanly speaking, only resistance and protest are possible. The light of the candles, ethereal and intangible, transforms their desires into a "yes" to "the days as they come." We are not so much dealing here with the chapel of a "saint" as with the school of divine love which has left its traces in the life of Titus Brandsma. The act of entering this "school" simply guides our eyes into the contemplation of God's love. Not a relic of a venerated saint but an urn filled with the ashes of countless nameless martyrs who were killed in Dachau shows us the tracks of this incomprehensible love. Established for the coordination and sponsorship of all initiatives which for numerous people inside and outside The Netherlands can make the memory of Titus Brandsma into a lasting inspiration is the *Foundation: Friends of Titus Brandsma.*

While Titus Brandsma trustingly made his way to a death sentence in Dachau, his research into Netherlandish spirituality and mysticism remained unfinished on his desk. Consequently the endless list of his publications came to an abrupt end. The rediscovery of the spiritual legacy of past generations and the courageous attempt to again make them available to countless "ordinary people" today thereby threatens to be lost. In 1968 the Catholic University of Nijmegen and the Carmelite Order decided not to erect a monument in honor of the former *rector magnificus* or fellow brother, but instead to give him the "honor" of a continuation of his great love for the tradition of spirituality. Accordingly, the Titus Brandsma Institute was founded at the University to give permanent shape to his life work in scientific research into spirituality and mysticism. After all, the questions which Titus Brandsma put to himself are still most relevant today. On the one hand, the research carried out under the Institute's auspices is aimed at making the riches of our spiritual inheritance accessible by new editions, analyses, and interpretations; and, on the other, at systematically increasing our knowledge of spiritual growth and developing strategies to foster it on the level of lived spirituality. By means of scientific reflection the researchers attempt to make a contribution to awareness of the God-relation and of God's working in humans.

Faithful to the concern of Titus Brandsma, they raise questions like: which blockages prevent the growth and awareness of the God-relation? And how can spiritual accompaniment foster the consciousness of processes operative in the God-relation? The study of spirituality can never be limited to texts and theoretical insights but will also focus on processes in which the spiritual way gains concrete shape in the lives of people. This research is not restricted to the production of books about spirituality but is ultimately oriented to the readers of spiritual literature in order that they may become conscious of their God-relation. It is our hope that this book, too, will make a contribution to that end.

Thanks are due to the many people who cooperated in the creation of this book. We want to make special mention here of Hanneke Veerman and Gijs Megens. By rendering their services in research, in reading out loud, and in writing, they offered support when a physical handicap began to interfere with the mental resilience of the author.

Hein Blommestijn

Addresses:

Titus Brandsma Kapel, Keizer Karelplein 19, Nijmegen
Stichting Vrienden van Titus Brandsma, Stijn Buysstraat 11, 6512 CJ Nijmegen
Titus Brandsma Instituut, Erasmusplein 1, 6525 HT Nijmegen

1. The Young Titus

Bolsward

There is an old photo of the Brandsma family which conveys a colorful impression of the many-sided richness of Catholic life. The photo, made at Beek-en-Donk, is dated August 15, 1905. On that day the family met in a festive mood because Siebrigje, one of the daughters, in a solemn celebration, had taken her vows and joined herself to the order of the Sisters of the Precious Blood. From that day on her name was Sister Willibrorda Brandsma. The parents are surrounded by their children. It is obvious that this event gives them a modest inner sense of satisfaction. Five of the six children have chosen the religious life as their life destiny. Each of them, however, wears a different habit and are not as unanimous as Thérèse of Lisieux and her sisters, all of whom entered the same Carmelite monastery. All the Brandsma children went their own way. That cannot have been easy for them. In that day family life was close knit and authoritarian. But a person has to come of age at some time and in order to reach that stage has to relinquish much that is precious to him or her.

On the photo we see the four daughters in the back row. From left to right: Boukje, the eldest, who had entered the convent of the PoorClares at Megen; next to her Siebrigje who had been admitted to her order on that day; then comes Gatske, the only married daughter, and to the right of her Plone, who had joined the Franciscan Sisters of Bennebroek. Each of these daughters had been conscious of the value of her own person and aware that, from that vantage point, her religious vocation could be understood differently.

On the left sits mother Brandsma. Her narrow face is framed by the gold and fine white lace of her Frisian cap. Next to her is Titus, the white mantle of his habit elegantly wrapped around his shoulders. He is the spitting image of his mother. In the center sits – self-consciously – father Brandsma. He looks straight at you. A man who does not beat about the bush. Next to him is his son Henricus, wearing the habit of the Franciscans. He resembles his father. At the extreme right sits Michiel de Boer, daughter Gatske's husband. Their two children are visible in the foreground. The family is not going to die out.

Years after the war Gatske remembers her parents as people of exceptional piety. On Sunday afternoons father Brandsma read to his family from Scripture. Along with his wife and children he loved to sing church songs which he accompanied on the piano. His mind was not restricted to his family and his farm, for he also felt quite involved in public life. He was, for example, a member of the municipal council of Bolsward and involved in the struggle for the recognition of Catholic schools. Mother Tjitske Postma was more focused on the interior experience of the faith. She was more inclined to shield the religious legacy and especially concerned to keep it pure. According to her daughter, she was a vocal proponent of Catholic isolation. She felt at home in the church which transcends all times, whereas father Brandsma was more involved in the issues of the day, in what had to be done, and in where the decisions were made. Mother Brandsma tended to be occupied with the timeless aspects of the faith, while her husband was fascinated by what is current and timely. The difference here is that between the seriousness of thought and the seriousness of action. Here lie the roots of Titus Brandsma's life – the beginnings of a new existence in which the current of life inexhaustibly continues and renews itself.

The Brandsma family lived on an imposing farm near Bolsward. The farm lay completely free and self-contained in the panoramic Frisian countryside. Its location is called "Oegeklooster," after the name of an outlying farm belonging to a medieval Cistercian monastery. There, on February 23, 1881, was born Anno Sjoerd who would later adopt, as his monastic appellative, the name "Titus," his father's name. He had great admiration for his father. It was said that he had much in common with him, while in appearance he of all the children most resembled his mother.

On the farm people lived in considerable isolation. In those days peace and intimacy were greatly valued. Work and rest were held in balance by the seasons, the feast days of the church, and the sanctity of the Sunday. It was in that close-knit circle of an introverted and soberly ordered life that Titus received his initial formation.

Church life played a clearly recognizable role in the life of the family. A person's church obligations were clearly defined. Numerous devout practices were maintained with seriousness and faithfulness. The images of saints and basins of holy water were designed to remind believers that they must continually sanctify their life. They built tall churches, churches which rose high above the rooftops of the surrounding houses. The church must be visible everywhere. Believers in large numbers made their way to it. People loved loud sermons, flowers, incense, and numerous burning candles. For the rest they favored quietness and inwardness. They did not want to be hindered in their attachment to the ancient treasures of the faith. This isolation was certainly not just caused by fear of being confused. It was also a sign of fidelity to the church which did not want to be of this world. Prominent Catholic leaders such as Alberdinck Thijm and Schaepman believed the church should not hide behind safe walls. It should enter upon the stage of public life and deal with the great issues of the day. They favored an open Catholicism. But not everyone was immediately persuaded of that risky idea. Throughout the country there were intense controversies over the pros and cons of it.

It was in that time of an introverted form of experiencing the faith that Titus Brandsma started on his life journey. At the age of 11 he left for Megen in Brabant.

Megen

It was still early in the morning. The first silvery light of dawn spread over the green countryside. On this early morning in September 1892, Anno Sjoerd Brandsma greeted a small group of boys standing by the streetcar stop in Bolsward and joined them.

They had their travel bags with them and stood ready to bid forever farewell to the small world of their childhood years. They wanted to become priests, as that was called. To reach that lofty goal they were going to Megen. Some family members came along to see the boys off. Local residents, with appropriate curiosity, looked from behind their curtains at the departing boys. And when they saw them enter the streetcar, where the boys, unconcernedly horsing around, looked for a place to sit, one of the locals would perhaps comment: "Do these little fellows really know what they want?" It is a question people can always ask afresh. For at this tender age the desire, though vague, is at the same time quite compelling. It drives them on – still unfulfilled and not yet burdensome.

The steam-driven streetcar, with its white plume of steam and smoke passed through the green countryside and disappeared in the direction of Sneek. There the boys took the train to continue their journey to the south. The still unknown future beckoned them. And in the old town things were quiet again. The quiet of centuries again took over.

In the time of the United Republic, Megen was located in the Free Seigniory of Ravenstein. Like the nuclei of Boxmeer and Gemert along with the surrounding villages and hamlets, Megen belonged to the non-state government areas. This area, where the quiet of an ancient past still prevailed, had a unique importance in the history of the restoration of the Catholic church in The Netherlands. At the Peace of Munster in 1648 it had been determined that in this area there would be freedom of religion. Here the monastic orders which had lost all their houses could again build their monasteries and study centers. The Latin schools of Megen and of Boxmeer were greatly beloved by Catholics living in the diaspora.

When Anno arrived in Megen and was enrolled as a student of the St. Anthony gymnasium, he was eleven years old. He had in his pocket a warm recommendation from the pastor of Bolsward, Wilhelmus de Keyzer. But the pastor did have some concern over his health. Anno was a frail little fellow and needed special care. He had a narrow pointed face; the boys called him "the point." In the stories about his years in Megen people were not able to detach themselves from the romantic cliché. He was the best student of his class, a little guy all of one piece. He was devout and wrote poetry. He received prize upon prize and was allowed, in the Sacramental procession, to walk with a lantern behind the priest who carried the monstrance under the baldachin. So much zeal must be rewarded, thought his educators even then.

The dark side is not lacking in this story. Anno had a weak constitution. He gradually became very thin and did not look good. When his father learned of this in Bolsward, he came speedily to Megen to take Anno home. There he would soon be healthy and strong again. Anno, however, managed to convince his father that he felt very much at home in Megen and that his skinny body probably had to do with his growth. Father Brandsma, his mind at ease again, returned to his home.

For the rest, what we know of Titus's early years completely fits into the image of that time. That image shows us a life and thought which displayed but little originality. The literature of the period is a faithful mirror of this condition. Poetry made much of rhyme schemes and alliteration. People felt very comfortable with stately, solemn sounds. There was a hunger for the sublime; people were decidedly anxious to avoid banality and coarseness. Especially in the hymns of that time people dealt lavishly with the sublime. This was not just due to a lack of good taste. It had much more to do with a need for certainty. Every renewal was a threat to this certainty. People wanted nothing to do with this unrest. They were content with the familiar and predictable. This lifestyle was deeply ingrained. People were profoundly attached to it. All risk was waved aside. Nothing could be allowed to disturb the peace. The entire education of youth was directed toward that end. The best means to it was the cultivation of respectability and virtue. The young people who were formed in the ethos of this virtuousness and could view it as ideal would never become troublemakers.

To apply oneself to imitation was more important than to cultivate one's own creativity. People attached much value to being a good example. The children's books of that time are full of it.

Originality was "out" and the example of successful persons was "in." In this ideal image many people found the certainty they missed everywhere else. It is remarkable that of the five children of the Brandsma family who opted for the religious life each went his or her own way – of all things in *this* period.

From Titus's time in Megen, finally, we also know something about his character. His fellow students said that even then already he was "somebody." He had a stable character and a well-balanced mind. That was his nature, a nature which had additionally been fortified by the close and well-ordered family life on the old farm.

Boxmeer

After his period of study at the junior seminary of the Franciscans at Megen Titus opted for the Carmelite order. His parents did not understand this at first. It was natural, after all, for Titus to continue on the path he had chosen and to become a Franciscan. Titus, however, believed that the office of priest or of an itinerant preacher would be too heavy for him. On the other hand, there had sprung up in him a strong interest in Carmelite spirituality. He felt powerfully drawn to the mystical side of the life of faith. In that period he often talked with the young Carmelite Casimir de Boer, his second cousin. These conversations undoubtedly influenced his choice for the more contemplative character of the Carmelite order. In 1898, accordingly, Titus made his entry into the Carmelite monastery of Boxmeer.

When in Boxmeer a visitor walks down the Steenstraat, he or she will easily recognize the Carmelite monastery, although it is not particularly striking. The facade is severe and plain. This plainness is characteristic for the lifestyle the Carmelites sought to shape. In the 17th century, the time the monastery was built, people generally made much of the face of a building. It had to say something about the prosperity and special importance of the inhabitants of the property. Carmelites, however, were looking for an introverted lifestyle. Upon entering through the simple portal, a person is struck by the tempered lightness of the interior. The white-domed quadrangular passageways around the inner courtyard constitute an invitation to silence. The stained glass windows of Abraham van Diepenbeeck (1596-1675) contain depictions of the holy men and women of the Carmelite order. The splendid colors of these windows give warmth to the light of the interior. The rear wall of the building is totally turned toward silence. In contrast to the rigid form of the face of the building the rear side – invisible to the passersby – has a few decorative features. The arches above the windows made of ornamental brick and the half-round forms are typical for Flemish architecture. The monastery and the adjoining church are connected by a roofed-over gateway. The gate is built in Renaissance style and by its rich ornamentation contrasts sharply with the plainness of the building as a whole.

When Titus made his entry in the Carmelite order at Boxmeer, the prior of this monastery assigned a cell to him. This assignment is more than a housekeeping regulation: Titus is entering a religious community which has a history of its own.

At this point he discovered practically that he would experience his calling and destiny not just from a personal but also from a communal vantage point. The liberating and creative word of God comes to him via a community, just as it did in the years of his childhood when he received the words from his parents. In order to talk as adults did, he learned from them the words he needed to be able, in time, to tell his own story.

In the plain white cell of the monastery the young Titus looked about him with a smile and some amazement. From now on this would be his home. He was dressed in a brown habit which still clung somewhat uneasily around his shoulders. In the hallway, next to his door, hung the name of the occupant of this cell: "Titus Brandsma." Not surprisingly, he felt happy. It was the happiness of a young man whose longing has now been stilled.

From the very beginning his cell had a special meaning for him. No disturbing sounds could penetrate this place; only the light had access to it. In the reflection of the white walls the silence becomes even more intimate. Another light enters here, filling his inner world. On the wall of the hallway where his cell is located

Titus saw a sign which, in plain letters, read: *Silentium perpetuum* (perpetual silence). At first he may have thought it was a practical hint: religious live here; don't disturb them; they may be studying or praying. Soon, however, it became clear to him that the reference was to an important, new experience for him. It is adressed to him personally. This little notice concerning "silentium" meant for him that silence is a process that will initiate him ever more deeply into a religious reality and that this process is never-ending, just as the renewal of life which has now begun is a continuous process. This initial contact with a new reality is something he would never forget.

In his first letter to his parents, he wrote: "I do believe that God has called me here." In that letter he wrote about his cell and his daily schedule. Additionally, he let his parents know that he was happy in his cell as well as among his brothers: "It is a small room with a window. Located on one side is my bed (my straw mattress is comfortable to sleep on, I assure you!). On the other side is a book case and on the third a little table with a lectern on which I have put my little statues (Joseph has already been patched up!)." Titus describes in detail what he finds there – the things which are necessary to his life. This is the place where he is at home. In Megen people said of him that he was really "somebody." Now he is really "somewhere." His parents can form a clear picture of the place. There is a fixed spot, an enclosed living space, to which he can always return and where he finds rest.

Perhaps this description is an expression of his conviction that a person also needs to be distinguishable in his inner life. Then he goes on to describe what, for a religious, a day looks like. Needed, as a complement to the right place – a place where Titus can feel at home – is the right kind of time. In the religious life there is an order of time designed to bring about a balance between prayer and work, reflection and rest. When at fixed times the monastery bell rings, the monk who sat writing behind his table will rise and go to the chapel in order to pray there. Whatever he may be doing, he will stop and do what the rule of the monastery requires. Now he will pray. He must learn to live in the "now." He now prays or does not pray. He knows that much can happen if he totally concentrates on the "now" and agrees with what it demands of him. The cell, about which in his letter to his parents (October 1898) Titus said that he was happy there, will always be there throughout his life. He is fond of his plain cell; there he is focused on his inner experience. For him that cell is a symbol of a deeper reality. No matter where he is, he can be in "his cell."

Titus is happy in his cell and also, as he writes, "in the midst of his fellow brothers." It is a small community of young men who have jointly started a process of formation designed to help them grow into the monastic life. There has always been a special focus on this growing into the community. Among other things, sharing in this life means that the brothers share with each other their experience – experiences of expectation and concern, of loss and of hope. The surprising thing is that this "sharing things together" is never merely the sum of what has been joined together, but becomes an original whole. This outcome is not predictable: something new comes into being.

He describes his cell in detail; he is obviously at home in it. It is his inner world. He will be at home everywhere. "My cell" can be understood as the key phrase for Titus's experience of God's nearness. In the final phase of his life it returns – in a poem which became widely known in the post-war years. In his first letter he wrote about his cell and his fellow brothers; in his last writings what is left is only his cell, but again he writes that he is happy there. His cell is his mighty fortress, the ever-living wellspring of life. There he became familiar with God's nearness.

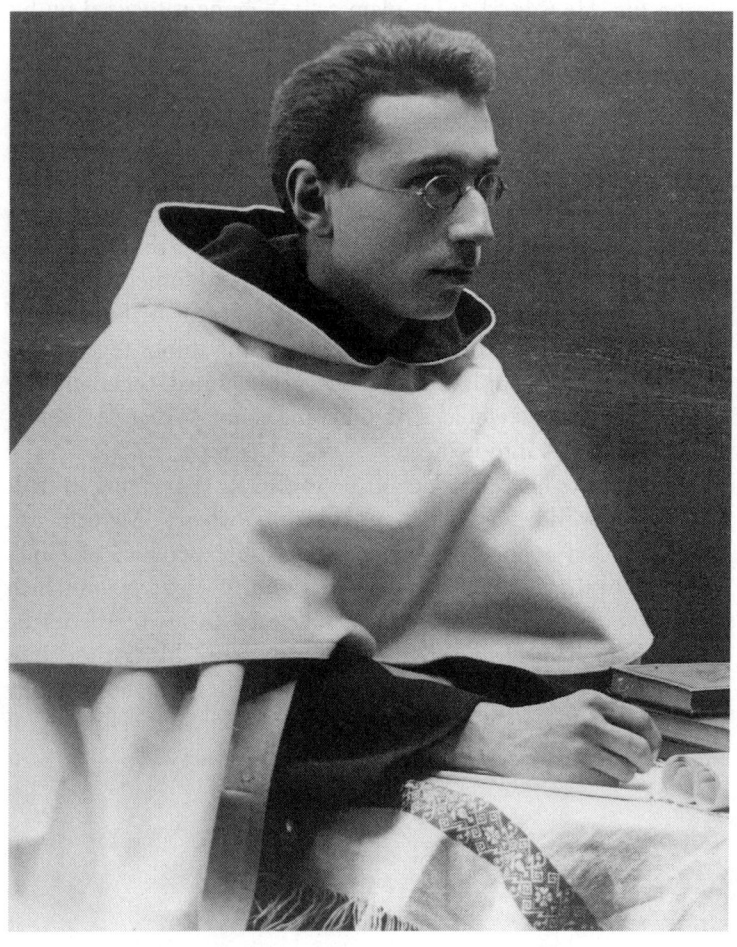

2. Years of Study and Formation

After Titus' novitiate, his years of study and formation began. He had been only briefly involved in this formation when there arose in him the desire to write and publish. His first publication is an *Anthology of Selections from the Works of Teresa of Avila*. It is a translation based on a French edition of d'Andilly and was published in 1901 by Malmberg in Nijmegen. This selection from the works of Teresa of Avila has a significance of its own. In Teresa Titus recognized something of himself. Of Teresa it was said that she could be restlessly at work without losing herself. Her life was far from easy. The Inquisition was powerful. Teresa had many enemies. She believed she was no match for them. Out of the frustration of feeling powerless and despairing, at the same time believing she had been called to something great, she rescued herself by starting from what she really was and could do. She said: "Being only a woman and having no status, I did not view myself capable of doing anything here of what I would have loved to have done to serve the Lord. So I decided to do the tiny bit I was capable of doing."

A half year before his death, when Titus was sitting in jail, he wrote that he was thinking of his old motto: "Take the days as they come." Titus is fond of these words. This means he feels a need to be in touch with reality. On the other hand, he is also very ambitious: he wants to do things that are important. His realism creates balance in his life.

In his anthology of the writings of Teresa, Titus selected the parts which concerned her experience of God. It is the subject on which he would often write later. They are the most penetrating and probing texts. Through his words the reader perceives that he was speaking in light of an experience he in all simplicity kept to himself.

We may take for granted that not everything in his life went smoothly. There is no biography that does not bear the marks of the horrors, the overwhelming nature and darkness, of the events in which people become involved. Titus, however, always kept mum about the most intimate realities of his life. There are only a few scanty indications that not everything in his life got off to an easy start. In the letter he wrote to his parents in October 1898, he writes: "I do believe that God has called me here, but please pray much for me that I may know whether I am following his holy will or not. And if by any chance he has not called me – which I don't believe or hope, however, since this life makes me very happy – that I may then know what I must do to please him." He does not start his monastic life with a predetermined decision. He must still get to know this life and find a way to measure himself against this new reality. In this context he does not wish to rule out the possibility that he might come to the understanding that he must retrace his steps.

Two years after his first publication, he founded a study-and-discussion club named after the Carmelite humanist Baptista Mantuanus. It is an in-house training school for science and literature. Again a few years later a periodical "Van Neerlands Carmel" made its debut. This enterprise still remained within the circle of the brotherhood. These initial "finger exercises" were intended to aid him in the discovery and stimulation of talent. The better contributions were published in national periodicals. An article by Titus Brandsma on Baptista Mantuanus was printed in *De Katholieke Gids*[2]. Hiding behind this classical author he criticized the lackluster character of Catholic life in The Netherlands: "Those who want to exert influence must prove they are entitled to that influence; those who strive to lay down rules for human life, to help shape society, to influence the general course of events, must be able to introduce material that is as good as or even better than that

---

[2] Baptista Mantuanus Spagnoli, de christen Virgilius, in: *De Katholieke Gids*, 16 (1904), 747-59. Signed: Carmelo Isebrandi.

of their rivals. This is how they secure the right to work together."
And in the *Dietsche Waranda and Belfort* there appeared an article
in which he developed a theory of beauty[3].

Titus was literally bursting with interest and zest for work. But
for a while he lost his momentum when he was told that he might
not go to Rome where – as he was told years before – he would
pursue his studies at the Gregorian University. His provincial superior did not feel he was up to it in view of his frail health.

When a year later the matter of his study again came up, the
objections were of a different nature. Dr. Eugenius Driessen, who
was known as an excellent but scrupulously Catholic scholar, found
him unfit on account of his "penchant for dangerous propositions."
He was then given some administrative work and made his peace
with it. When after some time the "climate" around Titus changed,
it was made possible for him to pursue his scientific formation in
Rome.

Sometimes it seemed as if the profound certainty out of which
Titus lived was a gift; there was no indication of the toilsome long
road required to achieve it. Many years later (1939), in a very personal contribution to a *Liber Amicorum* presented to Hubertus
Driessen on the 50th anniversary of his priesthood, Titus wrote:
"... that he was a stubborn man. Here and there I entertained
some opinions of my own which differed from those taught in the
school." Earlier already, in 1937, he wrote to the same Hubertus
Driessen that at the time he had made clear to his provincial superior "...that he [Titus] would not adhere to scholastic opinions
and that it might be well for him [his superior] to take serious
account of this in the event that in the future people would expect
traditional instruction from him." He ends this story concerning
the postponement of his study in Rome with the remark "...that
this was one of the many lessons I needed" and it seems as if with
this platitude everything had been said. Someone once wrote that

---

[3] De waarde eener schoonheidstheorie, in: *Dietsche Waranda en Belfort*, 2
(1905), 326-31.

the words which do not surprise anyone, the commonplaces we use almost effortlessly, actually function as calluses. They come up in the places where a person is most sensitive. He or she would suffer much pain and live life too vulnerably if these hard areas were not there. They protect us and, perhaps, conceal our wounds.

It is typical for Titus that he has told us little about this period in his life. In his own way he utilized that time and made it meaningful by occupying himself, undisturbed and with great concentration, with questions and problems touching his own possibilities and limits. In a situation which was actually useless and unfair and belonged to the dark side of his life, he immersed himself in the experiences of mystical writers, experiences with which he could truly identify. He turned his gaze inward: he was in "his cell."

After such a period of rest he would, with new warmth and receptivity, again turn outward. These periods recurred in his life to the very end. Activity alternated with silence, though sometimes it was a silence forced upon him by illness, which came suddenly and at most inopportune times. He did not experience this as contradictory and was able to take in both as meaningful, as meaningful as it is both to speak and to be silent. Both have their own significance and both are indispensable.

A Child of his time

During Titus's years of formation the Catholic Church in The Netherlands was in a phase of restoration. North of the great rivers the Church had been almost completely wiped out. The church buildings had been taken over by the Reformation; numerous monasteries had been demolished. In the second half of the 19th century the tide turned: freedom reemerged for the Church and a restoration was cautiously set in motion. This Catholicism-of-emancipation was marked by a serious lack of trained leadership. Catholics were found mostly among farmers and the shopkeeping middle class. Among them there were too few people capable of carrying out an important government function. Scientific education in Catholic circles lagged far behind. Another striking feature was the dominance of priests and religious. In that period they held all the leadership functions. Furthermore, people still spoke with a certain pride of the high number of religious and the many tasks they fulfilled – such as education, nursing, and care of the aged. In a certain year, for example, more than a hundred women religious were alive, all of them from the Bolsward parish.

It is striking to see how involved people were in this process of restoration and consciousness raising. It was a restoration of the visible church. All their attention was focused on the structures. It was of the greatest importance to them to see them function well. Restoration meant that Catholics would again play a role in public life; it meant hammering away at people's sense of duty, unanimity, and regular church attendance. Everything went quite well. The Church, to its satisfaction, acquired some status and had rapidly appropriated a style – one that leaned toward triumphalism – of its own. But it lacked the tradition needed for the interpretation and development of experiences which go beyond that which is concrete and visible.

In a discussion concerning the calling of the Carmelite experience Titus wrote: "The Carmelite order has a double goal. The first we must try to reach, with the assistance of divine grace, by our own labors and steadfast practice. That first goal is, simply put, 'to meet our obligations,' avoiding sin and practicing virtue in the process. But in addition we have been given a second and much more sublime goal, one we shall achieve only by a pure gift of God's goodness. It is that, not only after death but already in this earthly life, we will to some extent taste in our heart and experience in our spirit the gracious impact of the divine presence and the sweetness of the heavenly glory."[4]

Included in the calling to the Carmelite experience is the calling to the mystical life as a gift of God. Titus says very firmly that "… this is their first and highest calling which is not nullified by

---

[4] In this way he summarizes *The Book of the First Monks* or *Institutio Primorum Monacorum*.

any other. Therefore that foundation must be laid first and on that foundation we must build further. From this it also follows," writes Titus, "that from the moment they have been admitted to the Order the novices must apply themselves to an intimate and deeply spiritual life and not be admitted to activities of any kind whatsoever unless that foundation has been laid."

Titus felt very much at home in this period of restoration and advancement. A movement had originated which inspired him. At the same time he saw that something more was needed. He noted that many believers had begun to move. They were eager to join Catholic organizations. The meetings were well-attended. The churches were filled to overflowing. Usually, however, the focus was on the visible side of things: the high towers, the loud-sounding church bells, the festive liturgies, and everything that had to do with luster and power. Part of this picture is the familiar feeling of assurance and security, of being on the march as a body for a good cause. However, there was only little interest in the interior life of faith. In those days people were not sensitive to the inner depth of the posture of faith, a depth which can take people to less familiar but powerful experiences. One can describe this inner posture in many different ways. It is the mystical dimension of the life of faith, a dimension which has a rich past. But at this time people barely spoke of it. One can even speak of an anti-mystical atmosphere. In the institutional church there is frequently a tendency to – as much as possible – formulate the experience of faith in laws and uniform regulations. As a rule this results in a loss of personal responsibility and the rise of the religious type of the submissive and docile believer. Not infrequently those who excel in this respect are awarded papal honors.

Inasmuch as people found the phenomenon of mystical experience quite confusing, they judged it was not something for the ordinary person. As long as the mystical life was restricted to an elitist group, the Christian life would remain orderly and manageable. Given this outlook, the life of faith was no longer understood in light of experience but in terms of theology and morality.

In this period Titus Brandsma became increasingly convinced that mystical élan is indispensable to a true recovery of the church. He began to look for ways to witness to this reality. He lived and labored totally in light of this inspiring idea. He called it the foundation of his calling. On that basis he spent and extended his life in a great diversity of projects and tasks. However extensively his life developed in ramifications of a divergent nature, everything was fueled by the same inspiring idea. Wherever he might find himself – in a lecture room or on a train – and however much time people demanded of him, he never allowed himself to be sidetracked. He was driven by an enthusiasm which was ceaselessly propagated and ceaselessly purified.

Titus took great pleasure in playing an active role in this process of Catholic emancipation. He felt at home in the busyness engendered by the process, a process which gained momentum especially in the first quarter of the 20th century. People with great ideas about consciousness-raising and renewal were in the limelight. It was time to break with the petty atmosphere of the inner chambers to which Catholics had for a long time withdrawn. The resonance in the country was strong. Many things were set in motion. Hope for new and original times broke out. It was the time of the Kayotters and the Grail, choral readings and choral dances. Ariëns and Poels fought for better wages, better working conditions, and better housing. De Witheer Gerlacus van den Elsen worked for the emancipation of Catholic farmers and market gardeners. Schaepman took the lead in political consciousness-raising. Titus Brandsma concentrated on the development of the culture of the spiritual life and worked for the revival of the spiritual tradition. In virtually all areas of life there was a wave of activity.

The Frisian Homeland

Titus's great love for Friesland prompted him to be especially active there. He was very fond of the Frisian language. Wherever he might be in the country, when he met Frisian friends he spontaneously began to speak with them in Frisian and the spark of kinship would leap. On one occasion, in the city of Dokkum, Titus delivered a sermon in Frisian before a large gathering of pilgrims. The archbishop, who was present at the time, did not understand a word of it and let Titus know that it was not appropriate to preach the Word of God in a regional language. Titus replied that, given another opportunity, he was entirely willing to preach his sermon in Frisian again.

Friesland is a land of dykes and "terps" [mounds of refuge in times of floods], always threatened by water. There is much silence there but people also know of violence. The people of this province are familiar both with struggle and with the need for vigilance. Titus was particularly interested in the colorful history of it. He knew it takes much effort and planning to protect the riches of the past and to rediscover its original vitality.

In the meantime, also others had caught the spark of interest in Friesland's past. In the winter of 1916-1917 "It Roomsk Frysk Boun" [The Catholic Frisian League] had been started by Jouke van der Way and Johannes Rypma. When this League started its official career Titus became its Secretary. Its purpose was "…to unite all Catholic Frisians, both men and women, in the bond of friendship." For centuries Catholic Frisians had been a negligible minority. But now, for the first time, with touching modesty, they were stepping into the limelight. They were farmers and merchants. Government functions were beyond their reach. Consequently, among them as well as in the rest of the country, there was a great dearth of higher education. A "bond of friendship" was probably within their reach. If they were ever to play a role in public life, there had to be a bond of unity among them. That bond was a necessary condition for what lay ahead. Then comes the "more." At the celebration of their first lustrum it was established that the League had accomplished little. That is hardly a pleasant announcement to make or to hear at a festive gathering. Soon, however, the liveliness returned when the question concerning the reason for this plunged those present into a mild state of confusion. Some pointed to the younger generation: their absence hardly motivated the older generation. Chairman Hettinga mentioned the parish priests and chaplains as the reason: he had expected more cooperation from them. But, according to Titus: "...one must have a lot of patience with them."

In Friesland there were a number of societies with a more restricted focus – archaeological and cultural-scientific work groups – which Titus joined. Among them were a society for the study of Frisian history, antiquity, and language called *It Fryske Gea* ("The Frisian Landscape), the Provincial Advisory Council for Education, and the "Fryske Akademy" (the organ for the study of what is peculiarly Frisian in history and the popular temperament). Membership in so many groupings cannot simply be attributed to Titus's passion for work. His membership must have given these institutions the much-needed gravity.

When the "Rooms-Fryske Boun" had outgrown the difficult years of its beginning, the time was ripe for a new concentration of forces. Titus Brandsma, along with a few other well-known Frisians, launched the organization called *Frisia Catholica.* In 1937, under the chairmanship of Titus Brandsma, it took off, defining as its goal: "to advance, in the broadest possible sense, the cultural elevation of the Catholic-Frisian part of the nation by increasing knowledge of our Frisian past." At about the same time a periodical by the same name made its appearance. Titus's interest especially concerns the riches from the time before the Reformation. He delivered a number of lectures about prereformational Friesland, in which he deals among other things with Pater Brugman as orator and poet; Frisian monasteries, the oldest Cistercian abbey "Claercamp"; the monastery "Ferwerd"; Saint Willibrord in Friesland; and Our Lady of Friesland.

In 1925, in the city of Dokkum, the national St. Boniface Fraternity was again installed. Titus, being on the Board, immediately conceived plans for this organization. In the first place, the people here should see to it that the spring will again produce pure water. In tradition the spring or source has always been a symbol of ever-flowing vitality. Here, at this source, lies the origin of the Christian faith in the Low Countries. The spring, which since then has never stopped flowing, is the image of that origin, the pure beginning.

On Monday, August 23, 1926, the first national pilgrimage to Dokkum took place. Two thousand people participated, among them the archbishop of Utrecht and the bishops of Mainz and Fulda. At the end of the decade of the thirties, the procession park located near the spring acquired a number of stations of the cross. Jacob Maris, the well-known sculptor from Heumen, designed the fourteen stations. Titus Brandsma, meanwhile, searched in the last remaining ruins of the Frisian monasteries for still-useable building blocks. With these old stones Maris then built the stations of the cross. By this means Titus sought, in symbolic and other ways, to bring to expression the bond with the past for which he had the greatest admiration. It was his last initiative. He did not live to see the completion of the project.

Professor Rogier, the Nijmegen historian, described the period described above as "the quarter century of awakening." It was a time of advancement with a special focus on close-knit unity and the voice – their own – which had been silent too long. In that time the church was obviously an inspiration to many people. The vigorous revival made a strong impression. The church, after all, was the image of inviolability: hopeful times were about to dawn. Great certainty prevailed concerning the church: *it was built upon a rock.* All church-going persons, to their reassurance, had regularly and with strong emphasis heard this from the pulpit. External luster was not the only thing that fascinated them. The church was holy and elevated above all else in human culture, because the Lord himself continued to indwell it. People experienced this as a great mystery, convinced that here lay the power which brought them together. Catholics did not see themselves as solitary individuals but knew themselves to be united in a holy community. Associated with this sense of themselves is that they viewed it as the highest virtue to faithfully follow and be obedient to authority.

These were good times for the institution. It is typical for that day that people spoke more about the church and about Catholicism than about Christianity. This consciousness remained dominant in the spiritual climate of that time despite the intramural criticism which simultaneously asserted itself and was frequently not gentle.

In all these activities in the area of Catholic emancipation, activities in which Titus was involved on a large scale and to generate which he in many cases took the initiative, the renewal of the spiritual life of Dutch Catholics was his primary objective. This was typically his outlook on Catholic emancipation.

Surveying the activities of Titus Brandsma, one is astonished at how numerous and divergent they were. It is understandable that not everybody was elated about this. One often encounters this excessive activity in the leaders of the Catholic emancipation movement. One will certainly come closer to Titus Brandsma's world, however, if one digs deeper into the unfathomable forces by which his life was sustained. Over and over in history one witnesses the mysterious event that the living God communicates himself in abundance. Persons touched by this abundance of grace will also themselves be caught up in an abundance of activity in their life.

3. Exposure to Life in Its Fullness

Nijmegen: Professor in the history of philosophy and mysticism

In this period of rapid developments in Dutch Catholicism, Titus Brandsma was appointed a professor at the newly-founded Catholic University of Nijmegen. The time was June 1923. His assignment was to lecture in the history of philosophy and of mysticism, particularly Dutch mysticism. Titus wrote professor Hoogveld that from then on he was happy to apply himself to scholarship. He saw the necessity of scholarly formation if Catholics were to participate as equals in the discussion of current developments.

In judging Titus Brandsma's work at the University of Nijmegen, one must start with this motivation if one is to do justice to him as a scholar. His primary purpose was not to build a big reputation for himself in the scholarly world. His goal was above all to introduce as many people as possible into that world. They had to be molded into persons who had all the skills needed for leadership and for bearing responsibility in the life of society. Timeless scholarship was not his "bag."

As scholar Titus Brandsma was a son of his own people, easily recognizable by the typical possibilities and limitations of the Dutch as a nation.

Says Johan Huizinga in *Nederlands Geestesmerk:* "We leave all the windows of our house wide open and let the sea wind and land winds freely blow through them. We have become familiar with the temperament of other people and have managed to assimilate different cultures".[5] As a philosophy professor, Titus Brandsma came close to fitting this description. He was – as that is called –

---

[5] *Verzamelde Werken* VII, 1950, 291.

an eclectic, someone who does not tie himself down to a system but selects and gathers the valuable materials of others. Professor Sassen has demonstrated that this typically Dutch temperament has most clearly manifested itself in philosophy. Associated with this temperament, he says, is "... relative independence with regard to bookish teaching and the authority of teachers." Sassen then goes on to say that the Dutch thinker has a strong need for religiosity and mysticism. In that case he is working with things that are known to him from experience. All the indications are that it fits the personality of Titus very well to develop in that direction.

When he spoke of the mystical life his words became livelier. He knew that he was then speaking of things of which it is assumed that they go beyond the reach of ordinary people but of which he himself was convinced that they belonged to real life and were even an essential facet of it. This was his strong side and it's not surprising that precisely in this area he would achieve real growth. The study of mystical writers became one of the central themes of his life. This bent also affected his choice of subjects and his approach to them. He had a preference for the medieval philosophy of the Low Countries. "Dutch philosophy before the Reformation" was the theme for the academic year 1924-1925.

From 1927 on Titus Brandsma lived in a spacious house on the Kronenburgersingel. Across from the house was a green park. From his study, looking through the tall trees, he could see the weathered colors of the ancient city walls. They were for him an indestructible reminder of the eternal search for protection of the vulnerable life of humans.

Titus felt deeply connected with a magnificent past. Everyone knows that for him that was not a matter of escape; he loved his own time; he was surrounded by it on every side and saw numerous possibilities. But he was equally fascinated by the vital forces of the past – forces which are most essential to the human mind but which, as a result of the instability of the times, have largely disappeared from people's mind.

The spiritual heritage of the Low Countries

From the beginning of his religious life Titus made a study of the old spiritual writings. He immersed himself in the experiences of the mystical authors. It must have become increasingly clear to him that one can find there an essential answer to the questions of this time and that by our immersion in these authors the feeling that humans are the playthings of unknown forces and circumstances can be removed. Titus was an optimist about life. The pioneering role suited him very well. He worked on new ideas and new ways of doing things but was at the same time convinced that it is not possible to forge new ideas apart from the past. There is a kind of connectedness between human experiences and human expectations. Conscious of this inexhaustible mystery of life's connectedness, he worked hard to trace the spiritual influences which determine the unique character of Dutch piety. In his opinion, the life pattern embodied in Middle Dutch spiritual literature makes possible a new answer, one which a technologically-controlled world cannot provide.

His study of mysticism was a kind of dialogue with the past, a creative encounter with a rich experience. This study began with Hadewich, an unexpected high point in spiritual literature. After that he broadened his focus toward various currents which are characterized by warmth and clarity, sometimes spontaneous and impassioned, then again more reflective and sober. Titus uncovered the lines which point to a uniquely Dutch spirituality characterized by a network of interconnected motifs dominated by the central idea that God is inexpressibly near to us in this world. "If the Netherlands wants to recapture its earlier spiritual health, its people must again become conscious that to believe in God is the same as to live in God. We too must learn from our ancestors the intense fervor with which they related to God in the most intimate and confidential terms. They spoke with him in all confidentiality; they listened confidentially. In consequence, life takes on a different look," wrote Titus.

He did not study the mystical writers with the cold eye of scientific detachment. In him you do not find an anemic intelligibility but a constant personal involvement which comes to expression in an abundance of traditional formulas. If one irons out the solemn wrinkles, one is left with a clear and warm story. He was like the medieval persons of whom Guardini says that they, in meditation, immersed themselves in the truth. For these people the sense of being spoken to was very strong.

The high point in Middle-Dutch spiritual literature, for Titus Brandsma, occurred in John Ruusbroec, with his illustrious mysticism. In a lecture on Ruusbroec we read how he had been especially impressed by his balance. Titus calls him "the leader of Dutch mysticism who in his life, sermons, and writings united, in an admirable way, the theoretical with the practical. Now this is precisely the problem of our time: our life and our work have been split apart. They are not sufficiently focused on each other and do not form an integrated whole. This is true on every level of life; the economic activity of people is not rooted in their social world. When Titus repeatedly harks back to this subject, it is not to glorify the past, an attitude that is often a sign of rejecting the present and not wanting to bear responsibility for it. No: Titus loved his own time, for all its suffering and problems. He gave his life for it. At issue for him was reality, a better world, an ideal situation, in which there is a greater possibility of unity. There was a time in which there were no "merely" social and economic laws, a time in which faith was not yet separated from the other aspects of life. Titus's appreciation for Ruusbroec had much to do with his own life, perhaps even with his inner struggle and uncertainty. He, too, after all, was searching for a way of living which could impel the tension between "old" and "new," between tradition and the desire for originality, to mature into a new and fruitful balance. This theme of "balance" or "equilibrium" frequently surfaces in his writings.

Thus Titus, who was so convinced of the special significance of his own Carmelite spirituality, said in a chapter speech: "The ideals of an order are attractive to the degree that, in harmony with other ideals, they depict the riches of the Catholic life."

Sometimes it seems that in his own world of ideas he was running ahead of the facts. In a radio address on the topic

"Mysticism in The Netherlands" he made the statement that "...the artificial separation between grace and life, faith and good works, reflection and apostolate is beginning to break down. Our composite human nature is again beginning to discover its unity in God."

In the spring of 1931, in a preliminary report for the Catholic society on science, he wrote about his own scientific research into the nature of Dutch philosophy. "It consists," he says, "in looking at the world without being able to limit itself to that world and with the strong desire to see the relations to God in that world and to bring those relations to expression in a well-reasoned 'practical' life. Perhaps it could be briefly described by saying that Catholic philosophy makes itself known as an attempt to achieve a practically reasoned union between a sense of reality and a view of God."

Titus Brandsma devoted 75 percent of his total lecture output to philosophy. This proportion is contrary to the image of Brandsma sketched by the Nijmegen historian Rogier. In it he gives the impression that Titus took great pains to study the history of mysticism but neglected philosophy[6] which was his main assignment. Sometimes such a mistaken image can linger for a long time.

We can hear the motivation for his scientific work coming through at the time when the periodical "Ons Geestelijk Erf" [Our Spiritual Inheritance], a quarterly for the study of Dutch piety, was launched. In addition, the publication of a series of new editions of the sources of medieval piety called "Bloemen van Ons Geestelijk Erf" [Flowers from Our Spiritual Inheritance] was started. The motivation envisioned by the editorial board reads as follows: "Our purpose is not only to spread knowledge of the life and works of our Dutch mystics but also again to make their words heard in The Netherlands, audibly and intelligibly, in the broadest possible circle in order that they may again, as formerly when

---

[6] L.J. Rogier, Terugblik, 1974, pp. 15-17.

they were spoken and written down, bring inspiration to our people and draw it to a more intense interior life."[7]

In carrying out his professorial duties Titus Brandsma paid much attention, especially toward the end of the thirties, to the movement of the Modern Devotion. Titus had a keen sense of the spiritual riches available in this movement. This source, however, is no longer accessible. The Modern Devotion was a movement of "contemporary inwardness" which originated (ca. 1375) in Deventer around the person of Geert Grote (1340-1384). He castigated the spiritual decline present in the Church of his day and applied himself to the restoration of the life of Christian community. He founded new religious communities on the model of the first Christian communities. The men and women who lived by this model were called "sisters and brothers of the common life." In the early years of the 16th century this movement encompassed over 100 monasteries.

Mysticism is part of ordinary life

Titus was convinced that the seeking person of his day would be able to find a reliable route to the renewal of his life in the writings of the Modern Devotion. In the years between 1938-1941 he wrote a series of articles for these seekers in the daily *De Gelderlander*. In these articles he described, in a popular style, the results of his research regarding the Dutch mystics. It is characteristic for Brandsma that he wanted to share with ordinary people what he himself had discovered by study and research. In his search for the spiritual riches of the past he also undertook an important initiative which is still of great value today. It is a collection of photos of Middle-Dutch spiritual texts. He started this systematic collection in the summer of 1927. It contains a reproduction and documentation of spiritual texts from Middle Dutch literature. In 1938, in more than 170 albums, he assembled a collection of

---

[7] T. Brandsma, "Bloemen van ons Gestelijk Erf," in: *Ons Geestelijk Erf* II, 1928, p. 19.

16,000 photos of texts from around 60 manuscripts. This "Brandsma collection," as it is called, is administered today by the Titus Brandsma Institute at Nijmegen.

To Titus Brandsma, one can find faith – in whatever faulty form and impoverished state it may be – among ordinary people, the humble ones who live without great expectations. However high and noble our longing may be, ultimately it must concern something that in its essence is very simple: the mystery of God's nearness which, though unfathomable, can be experienced simply in a timid and tentative faith.

Godfried Bomans, in his own way, once captured the image of Titus, a snapshot of a professor, contending, thoughtful, with restrained gestures, ready to withdraw into himself. Bomans is a typically Dutch writer; he sees details and accidental features as a Dutch painter sees them. "The only gesture he allowed himself was the typical gesture of the right hand, the tips of whose thumb and middle finger were brought together as he was making his points. If one does this with the thumb and the index finger one creates a schoolmasterly gesture that is not without pedantry."

When Titus spoke about mysticism Bomans saw another man: "At this point the disadvantage of improvisation, which marked his purely philosophical lectures, completely disappeared to make way for the deep accents of a man who most powerfully embodied the material in his own person. I see Brandsma before me: his eyes fixed over our heads on the remote horizon of the almost inexpressible, the soft somewhat monotonous voice groping for the clarity and distinctness of Descartes which was so dear to him. His finely-sculptured spiritualized little head again appears before me in the frame of the window which looked out upon the garden which had gone to seed." These words of Bomans clearly show that when he listened to the discourse of Professor Brandsma he infallibly sensed that Titus's words did not proceed from academic theories but had to do with his own experience. It is fascinating to listen to someone who can speak from within the wellsprings of life today.

The mystic has seen deeper and richer depths of life than non-mystics. Actually he can only speak of these depths in images. It is an experience that can only be accessed from within. It is therefore hard to describe. It is possible, however, to say something about the road he travels. His attention is focused inward. He goes beyond the variable image of the world and of himself in search of the mysterious reality that is hidden behind everything. The road inward does not lead to inner solitude but the realization of living before the face of him for whom nothing is hidden. But there is something more. It is this Hidden One who sustains the life of the mystic and does not drop him. Increasingly he is touched more deeply by this thought. He becomes conscious of inner change. A new consciousness grows; he now views life differently; he also views himself differently and discovers his true self.

To his astonishment he now recognizes himself as never before. How can it be, a person asks himself, that somebody does not immediately discover his true self and that he has to go through a sometimes arduous process before he is completely himself. The secret of this is that humans are never so much themselves and never recognize themselves in their strength and their limitations as when they know that they are loved.

Years later, sitting in his prison cell in Scheveningen, Titus Brandsma was to write a short poem. In the opening lines he clearly expresses himself and explains where the source lies of his inner strength: "O Jesus, when I see you, I know again that I love you and that also your heart loves me...."

In Nijmegen Titus is soon known as someone whose piety is authentic and deep. People know him as one who has a deep sense of the mystery of the human, i.e. the religious, dimension of life, the dimension that is often too confined. The other person, to him, is not just someone who makes a claim on him; the other, with his possibilities and limitations, *is* the claim. His world is the measure of things. With the one Titus will go to the end; another he will furnish a good impulse to enable this other to go on.

Anton van't Hullenaar, Titus's neighbor, tells the story that every morning he had to take a two-wheeler handcart, loaded high with boxes full of clusters of bananas, from his warehouse at the Doddendaal to the railway station. "Just before 9 A.M. I would open the large gate of the warehouse and push the cart to the street. Across the street Titus Brandsma made his home. I would see him walking through his room. A moment later he came outside to walk to the university. The moment he saw me, however, he would wave to me, come toward me, and join me in pushing the cart up the slight incline of the street toward the center. That is how we, my professor and I, jointly went to our work – he to the university and I to the station. And that is what we did a couple of times a week for an entire year." On their way they talked about the serious distress and little sorrows of the Doddendaal. The people who live there are just ordinary folks, but sometimes they are struck by extraordinary suffering. Usually Van't Hullenaar knew somewhat more about that subject than Titus.

Do the scientific reflections of the professor still have any connection with the world of the hard limitations to which the man behind the handcart is subject? It is well known that numerous comprehensive studies at bottom concern something simple because they deal with the most fundamental truths of this life. Ordinary people can understand each other, and even find each other, in these truths.

In the Foundation Day speech he had given earlier Titus remarked that, viewed from the perspective of the most simple and unshakable truth, we are all walking the same road. A brief encounter behind the wheels which rolled bumpily over the cobblestones. Two worlds which touch each other briefly. The little world of the banana man where each day the same things have to be done at precisely the same time, and the world of the lecture halls where the light of the intellect affords seeking humans a bit of clarity on many questions. The hired man in the wholesale banana business lives in another world. In the world in which he lives and labors he yearns for another light, the light of the heart which can relieve his isolation. Only that light, when it comes down to it, can open up his inner self from within.

Titus deals with the students in a way which is remarkably different from the way he deals with the ordinary man in the street. It is his custom to demand more attention for the problem than for the solution. He lets his students join him in the search, gives them guidelines in pursuing it and for the rest believes he can confine himself to a brief summary of the results achieved. Some students had a hard time with that. Titus was probably insufficiently aware that what mattered to them was practical results in order to make rapid progress in their studies.

The students who had known him longer, however, understood his strategy very well. To them he was not the man who with rigorous vanity overburdened the other with his own knowledge of things. Instead of being the authoritarian professor, he offered the students space in which they could develop themselves and experience their study as a creative process. This is a striking trait in Titus; so much so that he tries to disguise by this ploy a rather spontaneously experienced weakness. Being easily marshaled to all good causes, it sometimes happened that he was deprived of precisely the little bit of quiet time he needed to prepare his lectures well. In that case, with unsuspecting simplicity, he made a virtue of this emergency. He had no need to exercise power over others. That made him truly receptive to real encounters. With such a person people find it easy to knock on his doors. This was something everyone knew who ever encountered him, the students of the university and the simple folks who, without money or employment, knocked on his door for help. He created the impression that he had nothing to do other than to listen to them. That serene inner poise came from a deep source. No one was ever able to disturb this inexhaustible source. That serenity was so consistent that, when he spent time in the concentration camp of Dachau, it also struck others. A Capuchin Father who was imprisoned with him in Dachau was astonished by "... his inner serenity and his smile while he was so battered that his teeth were knocked loose in his mouth."

Titus Brandsma belongs to the category of people for whom the times were telescoped. They view the events of today in the light of the past and the future. Accordingly, they see more than others. They are like prophets. The course of their life is not easy, for the more they see, the less free they are. It is not in their nature to compromise. They involve themselves radically and restlessly in the events of the day. They have to; they have no choice; they cannot escape.

Those who acquaint themselves with Titus's life, with the facts and events associated with it, will be astounded at the unbroken stream of conversations, plans, actions, travel, and meetings which made it hardly possible for him to find any rest. He proved to be indefatigable. He saw clearly what was especially at stake in that period and could no longer rest or keep silent. He was continually bursting with plans and ideas which often occupied him simultaneously and propelled him from one activity to another with a decisiveness which sometimes annoyed others.

One wonders how Titus could possess so much serenity and could at all times listen to people as if he had nothing else to do. We must perhaps assume that this abundance of diverging activities contributed to a situation where he continually discovered new depths of inner rest: those areas where no confusion penetrates and where a holy silence reigns. In that silence the answer keeps repeating itself, the answer which so much struck Titus. We hear the final echo of it in the poem which he wrote in the prison at Scheveningen: "Your nearness makes all things well with me."

The Idea of God

It is only in the last ten years that there has been growing interest in the inner unity in terms of which Titus Brandsma lived his life. The idea that a scholar cannot be a saint and a saint cannot be a good scholar is fading. The intrinsic unity in which mysticism and philosophy of culture relate to each other is the core of Titus's rectoral lecture on "The idea of God" which he delivered in October 1932, when he was designated Rector Magnificus of the university.[8] Central to this topic is the lived relation to God which, Titus

---

[8] Cf. K. Waaijman, Titus Brandsma, in: *Nijmeegse gezichten,* Nijmegen 1998, 53-59

argued, is the most effective counterforce against the fallacies of the time.

With reference to this lecture, Anton van Duinkerken – sometimes referred to as the last Catholic emancipator – wrote in the literary magazine *De Gemeenschap* [The Community] as follows: "It has become a custom of *rectores magnifici* of the University of Nijmegen to turn their occasional addresses into manifestoes whose content is of importance for the whole of Catholic public life. These speakers are clearly aware that they are not just speaking for the school but for the country as a whole. Ever since the address on 'A culture of our own' with which the 'Keizer Karel' university was opened by its first rector, professor Schrijnen, we heard things from that corner of the nation which gave us more than just the scientific information which, strictly speaking, we had a right to expect. The foundation day lecture of professor Brandsma, however, surpasses the important expositions of his predecessors in many respects, and even for the critic this is remarkable enough from a formal viewpoint. For this unadorned lecture was written in a language whose clarity not only compensates for its lack of aesthetic elements but also apart from them produces that especially poignant emotion which pure thought can give us and which in the way of aesthetic enjoyment approaches identification."[9]

In the opening sentence of his speech Titus Brandsma gave expression to what to him was a perplexing experience: "Among the many questions I ask myself there is probably none which occupies me more than the enigmatic fact that evolving mankind, intensely proud as it is of its progress, is in large numbers turning away from God. It is appalling that in a time of very great progress in a variety of fields we face a debasement and denial of God that is spreading like a contagious disease." Titus called this denial "the greatest of all human afflictions." He was disturbed, and did not understand it. The inner forces which move non-believers were

---

[9] Als werden wij bevrijd uit een ban, in: Titus Brandsma, Anton van Duinkerken, P.J.A.M. Schoonenberg, *God anders dan vroeger?*, Nijmegen 1969, 37.

foreign to him. The logic of their mind escaped him. To him it was an unfamiliar state of mind, devoid of purpose and hope. Titus Brandsma could not enter into the human fate of being locked into a life without perspective. When, therefore, he later ended up in a jail cell he was not overwhelmed by being locked up. He was to be there as in the open space of a truly authentic life and whatever might happen to him, he would draw his strength from the great expectation inherent in all things.

In the beginning of his speech Titus states that the denial of God must be counted the greatest of all human afflictions. It is remarkable that he, who usually had an optimistic outlook on life, was so somber when it concerned the question of God. He could not understand that people no longer experienced that question as meaningful. The German philosopher of culture, Romano Guardini, probably with a less acute sense of estrangement, saw how the question of God had bogged down in his day. He could, therefore, speak with greater candor about what a great gift faith in God was for him: he called it "this gift of all gifts."[10] But Titus Brandsma was disturbed. He saw and sensed deeply how much had already been lost.

Since the days of Titus Brandsma "the insidious spread of the denial of God" has not diminished. On the contrary: it has spread much farther than Titus could even imagine. Those people who despite all the confusion remained true to the faith they inherited marvel at that. For some of them it is a complete mystery. They see how people dutifully go to work in the morning, properly meet their obligations, and treat others with charity. They do all this, however, without falling back on the faith. They live with norms and insights they have discovered by listening to reality, by patiently absorbing their experiences. In this lifestyle one can no longer point to a religious dimension. Only that which has been culturally acquired impacts them and gives direction to their life. One can discern little sense of a religious meaning of life. When Fernando

---

[10] R. Guardini, *The Living God*, Chicago 1957, 83.

Pessoa, a man of his day, became conscious that he could not accept faith he wrote, "I consider life an inn where I have to stop over until the coach from the abyss arrives. I don't know where it will take me because I don't know anything."[11]

What matters most is that all those who are disturbed over this negation of God nevertheless remain clear-sighted and do not give credence to every confusion of the human heart. Unbelief continues to increase, almost self-evidently, it seems. Anything that is not scientifically certain can be calmly dismissed. Also where people remain faithful to the church and the ancient faith, the idea of God is impoverished and has lost its sparkle. "Oh – he is there at the end of life." "He exists as the One who punishes and rewards." "He is a distant God and a person does well to take some account of him."

We cannot turn back the clock of history. Present-day culture is developing quite independently of the religious dimension. This culture can no longer take us to that dimension. It will have to come from within ourselves and we will have to do it ourselves. Now that we are no longer invited and accompanied from without it is specifically the inner forces present which will make our life religious. Titus Brandsma puts it this way: "The indwelling and inworking of God must not only be the object of intuition but also manifest themselves in our life, come to expression in our words and deeds, and radiate from our whole being and behavior."

It cannot be said in advance what it is that gives us the possibility to have some experience of God. When, on his journey through North America, Titus spent time in the monastery of his fellow brothers in Ontario, close to the Niagara Falls, he wrote about the powerful impression this natural phenomenon made on him. At the end of his letter he comments: "I am going back again to the water which pours itself out before me. It is also an image of our human nature. This marvelous waterfall is visited by millions on account of its unequaled beauty. As for me, I most dearly

---

[11] F. Pessoa, *The Book of Disquiet,* 1991, 144.

love to look at the deeper foundation of this splendid natural phenomenon. Not only my eyes and ears are fascinated but rather my
intellect which reflects on what God has laid in the water. I not
only see the riches of the nature of the water, its immeasurable
potentiality; I see God working in the work of his hands and the
manifestation of his love."[12] In his foundation day speech Titus
described the development of the God-experience and interpretation through history. He concludes that in our view of God we are
bound to the currents of our day, especially the philosophical currents. The idea of God is not immutable like a rock but manifests
itself in our lives in ever-shifting images which do not mean an
essential change but place our idea of God in a different light. Titus
calls for great openness to this variability of the idea of God. We
must seek the Eternal One in time, which moves forward with
much inconstancy, dark and without much prospect one moment,
and more receptive to the holy and full of promise the next. In this
development Titus describes the mighty God of the newly con-
verted pagans, the royal ruler of the feudal period, the brotherly
God-man of the Middle Ages, the God of the 15th century whom
people served especially in outward ways. After that there came a
return to a more inward image. God wants to be served in spirit
and truth. Not the service of God was in the foreground but the
faith. Over against the familiar and all too good-natured divine
image there arose the severe and highly exalted Judge. In this
view God grew ever larger and farther above us. He became the
incalculably remote God. While he exists, we have no personal
relationship with him. He is "off the screen."

Titus Brandsma moved to the essence of his speech when he
stated "... that we must first of all view God as the deepest ground
of our being." He points out the way which makes this possible
for us, a way which will be surprising to many. Is it really possible to arrive at the acknowledgment of God by the way of
thought? When this is affirmed so positively, it must refer to a

---

[12] B. Borchert, *Mystiek leven*, een bloemlezing, Nijmegen 1985, 44.

way of thinking that is more comprehensive than purely rational thought. It concerns a way of thinking that turns inward. It is a kind of thinking that is not narrowed down, colored, and impoverished by defective or destructive experiences. Needed is the kind of thinking that has detached itself from this approach. The idea is a type of thinking that casts new light on our experiences and displays them in a broader context, a context which gives them a deeper meaning. It is a kind of thinking that is directed and fueled by the great inner forces of our human existence. These forces can confer a high degree of trustworthiness on our thinking. It is, after all, a kind of thinking that remains connected to life and consistently brings to our attention the truth of our life. Purely intellectual labor will not bring us to a vital knowledge of God. If a person becomes inwardly conscious of God's presence "in the ground of one's being" and if one opens oneself totally to him, he will make himself felt and work in our heart. He will shape us into a new human being. If in our thinking we become conscious of our inner capacities and let this impact us, it can lead us to the acknowledgment of God. These inner forces are, for example, the voice of one's conscience, our sense of being limited, a feeling for beauty, the hidden order in all life. It is clear that we are speaking here of an inner space, a reality greater than can be described with words from our experience of the visible world. Those who enter this world become more intensely conscious of their own life. It haunts them; they feel drawn to it; they want to go further, receptive to new experiences. It will become a long and dark journey. A person notices that he is bring moved and shaped by forces that come from the core of his being. As his attention for the inner life grows stronger, he will note with astonishment the great ease with which we humans admit to our consciousness precisely those forces which give us a positive self-image and confirm us too easily. We then view the world in light of this illusion. But if a person can manage to relinquish this illusion, no longer to look at the world through the filter of his own discretion, then his inner disposition will display itself and his own most essential possibilities will come to the fore. Once we have gone this way of purification, we will be able to distinguish more sharply which inner forces can introduce the right order into our life and make us into the person we want to be in the depths of our heart. We then understand that faithfulness, respect, acceptance, and integrity are the vital forces which place everything in our inner life in the right order and give us the sense that we are fulfilling our life in the right manner.

If we give serious attention to this inner world it will come home to us that the forces and impulses which set us in motion and guide us issue from another world. It is a reality which the moment we entrust ourselves to it and open up to it proves to be an elevated reality – also a reality for which no explanation can be found. To open oneself up to it is to experience it as a mystery. It is not from oneself. No one can acquire it by his or her own effort. It is given to us. It is as if the deepest core in us unfolds from within itself, just as a tiny vulnerable plant comes up out of the dark earth and unfolds from within itself. This tiny plant is a part of our world. It belongs to us, but we do not know where the viability, the germinating power, comes from. We have nothing at our disposal by which we can summon up this vital power. In it we recognize an essential part of our life which is the expression of what points to an ever-present mysterious reality greater than ourselves.

In the part of the speech in which Titus Brandsma discusses the idea of God which, as he puts it, "… guides and governs men's minds in today's society," he uses two words side by side: "indwelling;' and "inworking." They are cited in the same breath. They belong together, but not like a mechanism which has its own necessity. There is here an untraceable initiative uniquely its own. The "inworking" of God is the process of re-creation, the transforming presence of God. On this subject Titus says: "This indwelling and inworking of God must come to expression in our words and deeds and radiate from our entire being. We cannot exact from God that which he does in us. If we think we have some power over this sacred process, it recedes. God's Spirit blows where he wills."

The indwelling and inworking of God are the heartbeat of the religious. Whatever a person may lose in life, however heavy and sad his or her days may be, the heartbeat remains. For Titus Brandsma this was the most significant experience: to live in a holy inexpressible reality, the reality of "… the near, living God as the deepest ground of our being." These words have a special appeal for the seekers of this day. What they have frequently heard about God gives them little confidence and often makes them fearful; they do not know what to do with them. But the God about whom Titus Brandsma speaks is a God who wants to be near, uniquely present to people. He is the deepest ground in me where there is openness to him, where I can experience him – not in his fullness, but always only in part, not as a presence-at-rest, but as a continual coming in power. Titus has remarked that this idea of God is new for this age and at the same time a reflection of the representations of God from earlier ages. We recognize the same idea in a poem written by Teresa of Avila.

> And if, by chance, you do not know
> where you will find Me,
> do not wander to and fro,
> for if you want to find Me,
> you must find Me in you.
> Because you are My dwelling place,
> you are My house and home,
> and so I call out at any time,
> whenever in your thoughts
> I find the door closed."[13]

This image of God can remove much distrust so that the people of this age can grow into greater openness toward God. For God is no longer a power who breaks into my existence from without and subjects me to himself, but an inner power who impacts me in a liberating and clarifying way and causes me to look at the world differently.

[13] Eric W. Vogt, *The Complete Poetry of St. Teresa of Avila,* New Orleans 1996, 29.

Etty Hillesum, in her diary *Het verstoorde leven* ["The Disturbed Life"], writes about God in the same way: "That which is most profound and most rich in me, that in which I rest – that I call God."[14]

A human's inner world is holy ground. One must take the sandals off one's feet. It is the place where there is openness toward the infinite, the place where one really belongs. Sometimes one is expelled from it but one can always find his way back. It is what enabled Titus to be at home everywhere, whether in the midst of people or in the silence of his cell. He always remained conscious of the experience which touched him in the depths of his being and with which he was very familiar.

Also Etty Hillesum, writing in her diary in August 1943 from Westerbork, the Nazi camp, describes that experience: "You have made me rich, my God. My life is one great dialogue with You. Everything happens according to a deeper rhythm of its own. People should be taught to listen to this rhythm: it is the most important thing a person has to learn in this life."[15]

Titus believes this experience of God will appeal strongly to the people of this era. It is the most vital experience, one in which humans can recognize themselves in an unequaled way. It is an experience which will never lose its purity and power. When the violent events of later years came down on Titus in all their severity, he remained the Titus of this foundation day lecture, now purified by darkness and pain.

Anton van Duinkerken was so enchanted with Titus's description of God's reality that in "De Gemeenschap" he entitled his discussion of the lecture: "…it was as if we were set free." At the end he once more summed up everything in a single forceful sentence: "After his words it seems things look brighter across our land: perhaps for some this is one more frail proof that he understood the spirit of this age."

---

[14] *Etty, de nagelaten geschriften van Etty Hillesum, 1941-1943*, Amsterdam 1986, p. 549.
[15] Idem, p. 682.

An image of the world

In the summer months, when university lectures and tests were over, the days became somewhat more peaceful for Titus Brandsma. It was a good time to reflect undisturbed on one's own spiritual calling. In that time of the year Titus was usually invited to lead a retreat in some monastery. Over a period of ten days he then had to give conferences on the different phases of the spiritual way for which the religious had chosen.

When Titus had ensconced himself in the serene quiet of his cell he would lay a blank sheet of paper before him on his desk and sketch a hedged-in garden on it. "The Enclosed Garden" would be the title of his talks and with that the first page was complete. From this drawing, which looked like a Medieval miniature, would flow his descriptions of the things he found in the garden and the meanings he could discover there.

"The Enclosed Garden" is a familiar metaphor in spiritual literature. Basically its meaning is that the garden with its plants and flowers is a reflection of an invisible reality. Titus uses an image to make clear his view of the world of humankind. This has a special meaning. When he gave his lecture on the idea of God as that is current among us he spoke as a professor. He gave his address in the auditorium of the university, in the vernacular of the academy, a professional language. He approached his topic in a rational way. He appealed to the high appreciation there exists today for the human power of abstraction: "We live in a period of abstract views. This comes out in literature and perhaps even more strongly in the visual arts, the arts which are always a clear representation of what drives the human spirit. And it is that abstractive power which must lead us to the vision of God, the delightful contemplation of God."[16]

Now that Titus is speaking to religious we get to know him from another angle. He now speaks as the spiritual leader whose task is to give fresh clarity to the spiritual way the sisters are

---

[16] B. Borchert, *Mystiek leven, een bloemlezing,* Nijmegen 1985, 102.

pursuing. He had planned to make the sisters more aware of the fact that God created the world and sustains and maintains that world in an all-embracing order and that our life will only properly come into its own if we bring it into harmony with that order. He tells his story as someone who speaks from a deep sense of wonder. Titus knows that those who in humble faith do not seek out the grand and glittering diversions of the world but are continually prepared to relinquish the things that give them pleasure are most apt to experience wonder.

For the people of the university Titus Brandsma used rational argument to elucidate his subject; for the sisters he uses an image. In direct language he could not so clearly convey what animated him. The image he employs in many ways mirrors the world in which we live and at the same time brings everything – however complicated – together so that we can survey it at a glance.

The metaphor of the garden inherently exerts a mysterious kind of power. It is also charged with power, however, as a result of the long road it has traveled. For this metaphor we have to go back to the beginning of the creation. Its origin lies in the word "paradise" which means "enclosed garden." Enclosed in this word lies the eternal desire for a sound and unviolated life. However imaginatively one may describe it, it always refers to the world as it was intended. The image of the garden acquired a deeper, religious meaning in the biblical Song of Songs. Here we read with how much yearning and pain the bride sought her bridegroom in the garden. In the Song of Songs this love is of such high dignity that the bride and the groom are described as royal children. In this sorrowful search of the bride for her beloved, Teresa of Avila and John of the Cross saw the image of the human being who has perhaps been briefly touched by the mystery of God's presence and who with an unquenchable longing continues to search for his or her hidden God. From the 13th century on, in the movement of the Beguines, there arose a new cult of the enclosed garden. Up until that time the image existed only in literature but now it was applied in concrete living patterns with a more or less restricted degree of enclosure. The garden of the Beguines, with its little houses

arranged in an intimate circle around the silence of an herb garden, gave expression to the inward life. All threats and disturbances
coming from without were resisted. It was an image of balance and
inner serenity. Fairly many of such Beguine gardens still remain
preserved in the old city centers.

Titus knew the image of the enclosed garden from literature.
He also remembered how in earlier years he took walks with his
mother in the garden behind the barnyard where lay the green
pastures which extended toward the distant horizon. They took
great pleasure in the swaying ornamental plants, the purple irises
and the gossamer-thin golden yellow petals around them – a feast
of mutually reinforcing colors. The solitary slender stems, the sup-
ple compliant flower stalks, shade-loving rhododendrons, the
humble herb, the late-bloomers: all of life begins intact but vulnerable. The satisfied fragrances of the fall shrubs are full of
promise....

As these images rose in his mind Titus knew how he had to
begin the text of his retreat. He wrote: "We must turn our heart
into a garden." He also wrote; "We must make our heart into a
Carmel." To him the Carmel was the image par excellence of the
inner life. This first sentence was right on target. He sought to
transfer the sisters' experienced delight in external beauty to an
internal experience. As he finished writing down this sentence, an
inner world opened up to him, a world that is unlimited in its
beauty, held captive within the hedged enclosure of human life.
When Titus entered that interior world and wanted to explain what
has to be present there, he first of all needed to delimit the terrain.
There has to be "a deep moat around the garden as well as a high
wall." This wall around the inner space is my trust in God. If your
trust in God is deeply rooted, you have a strong wall around you
and you can withstand anything. In the wall there has to be a gate.
But this gate, the gate which gives access to your inner life, is of
all places the most vulnerable. It calls for caution; it puts you on
your guard. Who and what do you admit? "Only God and that
which pleases him." God makes his demands. But also the things
you admit apart from God make their demands and can introduce

serious confusion into your life. God, however, adheres to his purposes for you.

Titus walks into the garden and stops by all the plants as symbols of an inner attitude. Thus he describes a number of plants
and their symbolic meaning for the way which a God-seeking person has to go. He first mentions the sunflower as if it is his favorite.
The sunflower is the plant par excellence which testifies to the
secret which is pervasively present in the whole garden: an order
which does not have its foundation within itself. The sunflower
directs its wreath of golden yellow petals towards the sun. So the
humans who want to live a full life must turn to God to be filled
with inexpressible light. Titus now walks further into the garden
of the inner life. He becomes fascinated by its diversity. From it he
picks a small bouquet. The lily, an image of a pure disposition, the
rose of love, which can also wound a person, the humble daisy, the
whimsical sweet pea which has to be guided, the cut flowers whose
beauty is short-lived. The many colors belong together. These flowers do not have their beauty and fragrances for themselves alone.
They communicate them to everything within the space of the garden. The virtues of a human being give clarity and color wherever
they are recognized. They make life pleasant and trustworthy. In
the garden, amidst all the fragrant flowers and the waving branches,
along with everything that does not flourish and prematurely shriv-
els up, Titus knows himself a child of creation. In everything, however hidden, there is a spark of the divine. Thus he views the garden as a mysterious gift, the wealth of mature colors, the flower
that never opens up and is never pollinated. It is an order that is
given, a reality on which we cannot impose our will.

Throughout the garden, alongside everything that has been sown
and planted, one also always finds weeds. The Lord of the garden,
we are told in the parable, thinks that we must not pull out the
weeds. After all, one might also easily pull out the good
plants..There will always be weeds.

> The kingdom of heaven may be compared to someone who sowed
> good seed in his field; but while everybody was asleep, an enemy

came and sowed weeds among the wheat, and then went away. So when the plants came up and bore grain, then the weeds appeared as well. And the slaves of the householder came and said to him, 'Master, did you not sow good seed in your field? Where, then, did these weeds come from?' He answered, 'An enemy has done this.' The slaves said to him, 'Then do you want us to go and gather them?' But he replied, 'No; for in gathering the weeds you would uproot the wheat along with them. Let both of them grow together until the harvest; and at harvest time I will tell the reapers, collect the weeds first and bind them in bundles to be burned, but gather the wheat into my barn.'" (Matt. 13: 24-30).

The parable means that we can never separate the good from the bad. We will never be able to realize that which is purely good. We always have to deal with the bad. We do not notice it until it is there. That is the life structure of the garden. The flower opens and is pollinated and fructified when its hour has come. Weeds are destroyed when the decisive hour has struck. Everything in the garden alone or together with other plants looks in a capricious way for light in which to live. Creeping, winding around a stem, climbing up on a wall, everything seeks a way. Fragile stems look around them for support; trees bend patiently when the storm winds blow. The flower opens and blossoms when its time has come. Everything seeks its own space and has its own hour.

Titus saw that the failed plant which never blossomed, the dead leaves, and the weeds detract nothing from the beauty of the whole. Similarly the people who never bring anything good to a successful conclusion cannot take away the goodness of creation. The poet Gerrit Komrij agrees with this: the argument of the impious that the creation is full of imperfections and failures is not likely to impress an artist. That image will look quite familiar to him inasmuch as in his own process of creating things he has experienced so much failure and incompletion that "... can assume undesired and misshapen forms."[17]

---

[17] G. Komrij, *Over de noodzaak van tuinuren*, Amsterdam 1991, 11.

Titus Brandsma was not a man of half-truths. He admired the garden's beauty but also mentions the stones in the ground, the weeds and wild growth. Many people cannot accept a world in which all sorts of things are lacking. They only want to see the sun in its full clarity, says Titus. Its light is always there, but it is often hidden behind clouds. God really works in humans but in a mysterious hidden manner. God works in humans in such a hidden way that all that is human remains and is not destroyed. It remains visible, also the incomplete and misshapen. The misshapen and disfigured had little impact on Titius's world of thought. The purely good can never be realized; it is always "mixed." Ambiguities and enigmas will always remain. That is Titus's view of world history – unlike that of others who see criminality and suffering and question God's justice.

In this image with its numerous nuances we witness the attempt, but even more the desire, to give a name to the unnameable. Titus Brandsma, too, knew this desire to depict the search for God and all the unforeseen things one then encounters.

Titus was always open to people who had run aground in their problems. When they rang his doorbell, he shoved aside his books and had them explain why they could not go on. In these settings he saw that the divine dimension in humans is sometimes barely recognizable. It concerned him greatly when it dawned on him with how much brashness many people abandoned their belief in God and how small the gain of that liberation was. These people no longer have anything solid to cling to. They were completely thrown upon their own resources.

Titus could not fathom people who sought the meaning of their life and the fulfillment of their deepest desire apart from God. They were indeed capable of understanding things that were tangible and measurable and to develop technology to breathtaking heights. But, all in all, the meaning of human existence has not become any clearer as a result. As for himself, Titus was so imbued with the consciousness that human beings do not belong to themselves that his attention always spontaneously leaped out to him "in whom we move and live and have our being." That was his

– inviolable – reality. His optimism had nothing to do with what he would love to see happen, but sprang from his faith in God.

The garden is an image of the order of the inner life and the hierarchy of values. If one does not simply stick with the superficial meaning of the image, it discloses a connectedness which goes ever deeper and points to a meaning and origin on which humans have no influence. Although Komrij, in his Huizenga lecture of 1990, expressed some anxiety over the garden metaphor, he need not be afraid it will be lost. As an artist he looks at the garden from his own perch and arrives at the same view of the order as a believer. He observes that throughout the ages there has always been a very intimate bond between the artist and the garden. The garden is a reflection of a higher order, an order which has not been invented by humans. There is a time for sowing. No one can argue with that. One cannot speed up the time of blooming; every flower has its own hour. Sometimes the garden is full of seed-carrying bits of fluff; sometimes the branches bow down loaded with ripening fruit. There is a prodigal abundance in the garden. Without this extravagance the garden would be lacking in beauty and promise. This life structure is reliable; one can count on it. It reflects the inner structure. There is a time for reflection, waiting, and putting up with things; then comes a time for action.

It frequently happens in the life of humans that, when it is neither sought nor expected, a flood of human vitality breaks through. The time of abundance comes when the hour for it strikes. Titus Brandsma had a tendency to respond readily to someone who asked him for a favor. It was hard or him to say "no." But when the time of Nazi violence broke out his "no" was very firm. He traveled, he wrote, and he protested. In that hour of threat he did what was needed. Similarly, in the inner life of every human being, there are moments of waiting and receiving; and then, alongside of this, there is the time for decision, action, and self-giving.

It is the order of existence based on the truth that God is the Creator, the Lord of life, and humans are his creatures.

The deeply religious significance which Titus Brandsma saw in the world about him has now been almost completely lost. While many people say they still believe in God, they do not realize that their faith has been reduced to discussion material. They consider God to be a remote and strange being who lives in an unattainable world of his own and of whom one cannot really say anything recognizable. The fact that God is present in our world, that he is near to us and works in our life, remains foreign to them. Humanity and nature have drifted apart; the tangible and the spiritual, the human and the divine – each of these have acquired a domain of their own. Titus longed for a unity that is more than a matter of taking account of each other. He anticipated a unity greater than any human order. In the text of his "Enclosed garden" retreat we can discern Titus's longing for the unity of the whole of life. It is a unity which heals all the dichotomies and fragmentations which have occurred in human history. He longs for a better world image. It has to be an image which enables him to resist the falsification and deception of his day. Humans must again view the world in which they live with all their ups and downs as a single coherent whole in which they can discern an order which transcends them. In brief, it can be said that the unity of faith and daily life must again be restored.

In Titus' life there was no split between the holy and the natural or – to put it another way – between the divine and the human. The things of God and the things of humankind touch and penetrate each other. While there is a distinction between them, there is no separation, not a higher world and a lower world which cannot reach each other. There is a reality in which the holy and the human touch and penetrate each other. Titus writes: "… the divine is not only recognized by reason and accepted by faith but it also becomes visible, albeit nebulously, palpable, albeit under the always somewhat vague forms of self-observation. It is therefore hard to draw a clear line between the divine and the human.

In the case of Titus, the regional temperament that was his and the time in which he lived have a strong bearing on the spiritual formation he underwent. The things a person brings with him, the things he has acquired by dint of his own efforts, play a role in the spiritual journey he pursues. What he is by virtue of his own disposition and what he is given are intertwined. Incidentally, this is also the reason why the ideas of God in successive eras are so very different.

In a natural and sometimes spontaneous way Titus Brandsma lived in terms of transcendent reality, the reality of the holy and the divine. For him this was not only a reality in which you had to believe, but also a reality you could experience. Among other things this truth comes to light when we observe how real life is shaped and led by what we can understand and is rational but also by the accidental. He was especially alert to the interconnectedness between things in the world, an interconnectedness we have not constructed ourselves. The concurrence between the rational and the unexpected does not disturb life but builds it up and continually renews it. It is the secret of the living God who in his creative freedom is always new and different from what we expect. It is a secret that always surrounds us but which one can only experience if one responds and surrenders to it: if one does what has to be done.

An image of the human person

Some years later Titus traveled through the country to speak to students about developments associated with the ideology of national socialism. He wanted to warn them against the rising threat inherent in this ideology against a true image of the human person. Titus was very disturbed about these developments.

It was his conviction that the image of the human person which had emerged in Nazism was completely contrary to the way in which the Christian world viewed humanity. Compromise was no longer possible. This way of thinking had to be totally rejected. Central in his words is the theme of spiritual heroism. With a few broad strokes he pictured the ideal image of the human person and expressed the hope that it would not be threatened by a distorted Germanic image of the human hero. His text has the characteristics of a sermon: a mixture of the original and the cliché. To our ears such texts do not sound as compelling as when they were delivered in their own day. Add to this that ethical concepts, from a linguistic viewpoint, soon pale and lose their original vitality.

Titus was disturbed that any people were so easily misled by enthusiasm and power that they succumbed to external show and convenience without asking what was actually going on. It was a serious matter. The future was in danger. We may be entering a dark period. "The confusion is so great that everyone is gradually beginning to see that, unless a few people rise up in the power of God, unless something is done that makes a deeper-than-usual impression, we will irrevocably end up in a swamp. For that reason people are calling for a strong man; and for that reason people look with hope and suspense at all sorts of expressions which bear a somewhat fiercer character as a portent of the great deed which will bring deliverance. People are therefore speaking of a great era to come. We are therefore witnessing the revival of a hero worship which is not always healthy."

National socialism[18] needed heroes: people in whom the ideals of the movement became visible in a spectacular way. Strikingly prominent in these ideals was the dominant character. The serving aspect of life, on the other hand, did not sufficiently come into its own. In actual fact Western culture as a whole exhibited this pattern of the ruling person, a pattern reinforced by the rapid development of science and technology.

Displayed in National Socialism, however, there was an additional factor: frustration and a sense of powerlessness rooted in a lack of space for the development of people's own creative energies. This had the effect of unprocessed toxic materials. Some of these creative forces consequently turned into their opposite and became destructive forces with a potential to become demonic. "Their heroes," said Brandsma in his address, "are those who want to tower above others and so make an impression." By these words he meant to say: "That is all it is." It is banal. Their acts of heroism are aimed

[18] The ideology of Nazism.

at self-aggrandizement, having power over others, the unquenchable desire for more power. They have no concern for others; they
only view them as rivals. The personal value of the other escapes
them. They do not acknowledge the other and his rights. He is
trampled under foot and ultimately murdered. The idea of heroism, Titus continued, has never been violated more than in this
period: "The regrettable thing is that in this mental confusion people view as 'heroic' acts which in no way merit this epithet. We are
not primarily dealing here with the standard but with what is being
measured. The big mistake is that people are looking for acts of
heroism in an area where one must not look for them or expect
them."[19]

Titus then offers some examples of people whom he regards as
truly heroic. They are people who are filled with "… noble love and
who show more than ordinary courage in expressing it." He regards
as such a person Dr. Carl Sonnenschein (1876-1929). In 1918 this
Rhineland priest came to Berlin and over a period of a decade
became "the apostle of Berlin." "Do you want to know his secret?"
said Titus to the students; "listen to what he writes." "The religious
person is primary. Therefore let us pray. Second, however, is the
social person. You must help your brother. Without delay. Without ambivalence. You must honor the presence of Christ in him.
Behind all the mysteries of big-city distress, behind all the wildness
of big-city decadence, behind all the folly of these pagan cities is
the most profound reality of all: the image of the Lord, illuminat-
ing, commanding, fulfilling. Kneel before the presence of God in
your brother. Am I my brother's keeper? I do not know him, do
I? I have no contact with him. Yes: you are your brother's keeper.
Create contact. Christians join hands and act… *charitas*. Do not
ask questions. Do not look behind you. Do not judge. *Help!*
Unknown heroism. No billboard reports it. It does not get through
to people on the street. It does not cry out seductive slogans. But
it exists. In a thousand forms and figures the incomprehension,

---

[19] B. Borchert, *Mystiek leven, een bloemlezing*, Nijmegen 1985, 176.

the distress of human life, passes through the world. Therefore there have to be priests and lay people who still speak a word when all the words of this world are useless; who open a well when all other wells have dried up; who still have a sparkle in their eyes when all the stars have ceased to shine."[20]

The heroic person whom Titus champions is the person who sees the other, who does not leave the suffering to their fate, who does not shove aside the weak brother but respects him because he sees in him, as in all people, the spark of a divine power. When the other experiences this he can again believe in himself and rise up to a new life. Weakness reveals the mystery of the human person. Weakness and decline unmask our self-invented human image and lay bare the brokenness of existence. There is more in the world than money, politics, social status. There is more and that "more" is a secret. What is our true identity?

In a letter, postmarked December 1942, Etty Hillesum writes about the Nazi camp in Westerbork:

> On that infertile strip of heather of five-by-six hundred meters also the head honchos from the cultural and political life of the big cities wash up. All of a sudden, in one mighty gesture, all the stage screens have been removed from around them. Now they stand, still shivering and ill at ease, on that drafty open podium that is called Westerbork. Around their – displaced – figures there still palpably hangs the atmosphere of the restless life of a society more complicated than ours here. They shuffle past the thin barbed wire and their silhouettes shift in gigantic outline and unprotected against the vast plain of the sky. It is really something to have seen them go there.... Their well-cut harness of position, class, and possessions has fallen apart and now they stand in the last undershirt of their humanity. They stand in an empty space, bounded by heaven and earth, and will themselves have to populate this space with that which is still alive in them in the way of possibilities, for outside of that there is nothing. We now realize that in life it is not enough to be only a competent politician or a gifted artist. In the most poignant distress life

[20] Idem, 131.

demands very different things. Yes, it is true, we are being tested with respect to our final human values.[21]

Titus's deep anxiety over the "Übermensch," the distorted human image of Nazism, was totally warranted, as we learn from history. On Thursday, January 22, 1943, the Waffen-SS vacated the Jewish psychiatric hospital "Het Apeldoornse Bosch." In an extended freight train 50 members of the nursing staff, 900 patients, and 100 children – many of them barely dressed – were loaded – without food, without medicine, without sheets – onto freight cars from the station in Apeldoorn and deported directly to Auschwitz to be gassed immediately upon arrival.

Each person has value, also the weaker ones. Nowhere else in Scripture is this so poignantly expressed as in 1 Corinthians 1:27-29. "God chose what is weak in the world to shame the strong. God chose what is low and despised in the world, things that are not, to reduce to nothing things that are, so that before God no one would base his appeal upon himself."

[21] Etty, *de nagelaten geschriten van Etty Hillesum*, 1941-1943, Amsterdam 1986, 628-629.

4. Secondary Education

Beside his work at the university of Nijmegen there were two other areas in the Catholic community in which Titus Brandsma was deeply involved. One was Roman Catholic secondary education which was rapidly developing. The other was the Catholic daily press which had already begun to play a substantial role.

These are two important spheres of influence which so suited Titus's sense of calling that he felt totally at home there. To his mind he was working precisely where he should be.

His leaning toward these two tasks was very timebound. It arose from experiences he incurred at a time of a great cultural lag among Catholics. Titus had already gotten to know these two areas early in life. The school was the area of inward-looking life where people pore over books and try to appropriate the great legacy left to them. It stands for the seriousness of thought. Next to it was the world of journalism. It is the open space where crucial things happen and life takes surprising turns. It stands for the seriousness of action.

When in 1909 Titus Brandsma had completed his studies in Rome he was appointed soon afterward as instructor in philosophy at Oss, where the Carmelites had founded a school of their own. Rather quickly he turned out to be a driven person who felt a special emotional interest in people who in their search for truth and justice had been unable to find a solid frame of reference and place of protection. He, accordingly, did not limit himself to his lesson plans. He went out to see what was going on locally. In the course of his tour he discovered that in Oss there was a crying need for secondary education. In such a situation it was his nature to spring into action, to galvanize people, and not to rest until the right steps had been taken. The result was that in 1919 a secondary school for business was established in Oss. For a period of two years Titus became its head as well as teacher of mathematics and geometry. In 1923, after years of struggle, followed the opening of the HBS ("Hogere Burger School" – former Dutch High School for the 12-18 year age group), the present-day Titus Brandsma Lyceum. From that time on growing numbers of adolescents in the north-eastern corner of Brabant were able to get an education.

Also in Twente people came to the conclusion that there was a need for a Catholic secondary school. They believed that the city of Oldenzaal was the obvious place for it, seeing that Oldenzaal was viewed as the center of Catholic Twente. It is primarily history which gave Oldenzaal a measure of importance. Between 1605 and 1626 Oldenzaal was in Spanish hands. In that area, consequently, the church enjoyed freedom and protection, whereas in the rest of the country the Catholic church was prohibited. From the time the apostolic vicar Rovenius settled in this free city, it became an important Catholic center from which mission work in Holland was organized. And so it happened that, in 1923, in part as a result of Titus Brandsma's involvement, a Catholic secondary school became a reality in Oldenzaal. A few years later, in 1926, Titus succeeded in obtaining the requisite government subsidy both for the HBS in Oss and for the secondary school in Oldenzaal.

For Titus 1923 was an important year, not only because of the opening of the secondary schools in Oss and Oldenzaal but also because in that year the Roman Catholic University of Nijmegen (where, as stated above, he was to become a professor) was launched. Throughout his entire academic career, in the months of June and July, Titus would go into the country as authorized examiner to supervise the final examinations at secondary schools. Probably in part as a result of what he learned in connection with these examinations, Titus was worried about the deteriorating link between secondary and university education. Accordingly, when the Bolkestein commission was mandated to develop new syllabi with a view to improving the link between secondary and higher education, Titus became a very active member of the subcommittee for the historical and economic sciences. One of the recommendations submitted by this commission was to allow the HBS and Gymnasium students to work more independently to facilitate their transition from the secondary school to the university. In 1924 the Association of Roman Catholic High School and Gymnasia Boards was founded. Of this Association Titus was the chairman from 1925 until his death in 1942. At the start this was not a heavy burden. Each board acted autonomously and there were only a few common problems. After the 10th of May 1940, the day the war broke out, this changed. On that date a period began in our country which in numerous respects was not comparable to the preceding period. As we will see in a moment, this was also very true for Catholic secondary and higher education.

Titus Brandsma worked hard to get the subject of philosophy introduced in the secondary schools. He tried to bring this about, to mention one example, in the Carmel Lyceum of Oldenzaal. To that end he developed an outline for the study of philosophy adapted to secondary education. The reason, said Titus, was that philosophical instruction can only deepen education and help students to think independently and become conscious of what is essential in human life.

Reverence for the human person

In a speech delivered in Eindhoven on April 30, 1939, on the occasion of the anniversary of the Saint George college, Titus Brandsma divulged many of the inner motives underlying his activities in the field of education. At the start of his address he mentions the legend of St. George. For him this legend was primarily "a symbol of the struggle for the honor of God and against all evil." In this legend what appealed to him in particular is the idea that human beings must struggle. He developed this idea at length.

> There is no denying that the life of man is a struggle. Even as we celebrate an anniversary of this College of St. George, the idea of struggle does not go away. The college was born out of a struggle. I do not in the least wish to imply that it had to overcome opposing opinions or deal with financial problems. That is not the story of St. George and the Dragon. Those are simply the difficulties

inherent in the effort to strengthen people's love for the cause and to give it deeper grounding. It is not this struggle I have in mind. It is the battle St. George waged against evil in order to allow everyone to quench their thirst, free and unhindered, at the spring that was threatened by the dragon. It is the struggle which saves the child from the clutches of the devil so that it can quench its thirst at a spring that offers pure water.

In the opening part of his anniversary speech Titus repeatedly stated that the life of a human being is a struggle. He does not say that he has personally experienced it to be true. We may assume, however, that his personal experience resonated with this thesis. For Titus this struggle or battle is not something which makes a person afraid and from which he wants to run. Titus was a Friesian. It is said that Friesians are a militant people who love to be at peace. Titus always viewed struggle in the light of victory. St. George sat high on his horse and the dragon did not stand a chance. It is the legend of a sure fight. There is rest at the heart of the struggle.

In this speech Titus Brandsma explains why he thinks Catholic education is important. In making his case he does not feel he is taking a final stand with his back to the wall and must now invest all his energies in defense.

Let me be frank and say that I am opposed to action based too much on negative premises; that I have had more than enough of an exaggerated drive to fend off errors. In my opinion there is better and nobler work to do. We are losing ourselves far too much in disputes and defensiveness, in fending off error and fear of dangers.

However, before he turns to the constructive part of his speech, he wants to raise a number of fundamental points. We fall far short of our goal, says Titus, if we engage in education without speaking of God. Titus Brandsma's top priority is concern for faith in God. Thus, as we noted earlier, in his foundation day speech of 1932, he first of all highlighted his anxiety over the loss of faith in God: "It is appalling that in a time of very great progress in a variety of fields we face a debasement and denial of God that is spreading like a contagious disease." "When this is lost," he said, "the greatest evil has befallen us." It was obviously a matter of grave concern to him. He repeated: "There is no denying that leaving this factor out of consideration must deprive human life of something that ought to have first place in it. Thus our youth is deprived of that which is most noble and best."

Then, brick by brick, he built up the edifice of Catholic education. It creates the space in which the true hierarchy of values prevails. The young find here precisely the protection they need. "Religion has always been a factor of the greatest influence on the moral life of society. Life is controlled and guided by the first-order questions concerning origin and purpose." As he is gathering the building blocks, he cannot refrain from once more issuing a warning against a neutral education. He especially stresses that these dangers can so easily slip in unobserved. "They obscure the truth. A weak child cannot bear the harmful effects of such an education." He does grant, however, that one must be realistic: "Of course, you cannot bring up the young without running risks."

Now that Titus has again briefly vented his feelings, he continues to build constructively. In sum, the essence of what is at stake in a religious upbringing is an "education permeated by the truth which God has revealed, respect for his laws, delight over his work, love for his goodness." This, according to Titus, has to be the core of religious instruction. Though he has defined the core, religious instruction cannot be confined to it. Attention must also be given to "what, besides the classes in religion, lies hidden by way of religious elements in the different disciplines and consists of their most beautiful dimensions." Now that he has explained the essentials of religious education he points out what the result of it is. By its connection with God and religion education comes alive and corresponds to reality: its vitality becomes broader and it gains in warmth and inspiration.

In the first place he mentions "reverence." That has a special meaning. Reverence, after all, is something a person cannot acquire. Reverence is something that comes over a person. It can happen when a person finds himself in a mountainous area and becomes aware of the massive beauty of the mountains, or when a person peers down at the splendid detailed beauty of a dew drop. It is a beauty that has not been made by human hands. Present here is a mystery: it is very close, yet inaccessible. You cannot put your finger on it. Those who experience it are filled with reverence and awe. In this sense of awe persons of integrity feel that they are confronted by a reality that is not their own and will never be their possession. They reverence the peculiar beauty of the things they see around them and give them space so that they can come into their own. This reverence has a special meaning in Titus Brandsma's discourse. In this posture of awe, of a sense of one's own smallness, lies the beginning of a religious experience. One can have respect for others in many different ways. It can be their integrity, their faithfulness, their creative spirit. In Titus Brandsma's thinking respect for people exists on a high level. His respect arises from the fact that all people are connected with each other in and through God and by virtue of this natural order stand in relation to each other. This interdependence and mutual connectedness, plus the most intimate fellowship, must be the most beautiful thing that can be conceived with a view to rescuing people from the present distress"[22].

This respect for others induces a person to give his fellow humans the space in which they can be themselves. A space in which they are not exploited, where they are not left to their fate, where they fit. To make room for others means to step aside, to take a step back, be restrained. When someone does this sincerely and from pure motives, without secretly pursuing their own interests; when one so focuses on the other and creates room for that other only, then does the other experience what every person basically desires: to become completely himself. A space opens up before him in which he experiences a new freedom and can come completely into his own. And thus, after sometimes long and heavy sentences, Titus Brandsma arrives at his conclusion: "As a system our own religious education is to be greatly preferred over a

---

[22] Foundation day speech 1932.

neutral education; but sometimes we only let our Christian principles shine through so intermittently that people may well ask: is this what you are spending all that cash for?" What comes through in these words, as it did throughout the speech, is a high degree of certainty. It was characteristic for the mind of the church of that time. Titus was a devout son of the church, conscious that he was active in the name of an inerrant church.

Having brought his speech to a good conclusion, Titus Brandsma ended with a few comments which spilled over out of the fullness of his heart. These schools in Eindhoven, he said, can "boast of good results now that it is evident that we can work with the youth of that city and that there is genuine receptivity in them for what is offered here." This theme of receptivity is most typical for Brandsma. In his speech Titus had expressly referred to the receptivity of the growing child. Precisely at this point he drew in the parents. They can do a lot to awaken this receptivity in their child and bring it to a healthy development. It was completely in line with his outlook to make special mention of this receptivity. He wanted to make clear that people must not remain stuck in externals. They must go deeper to bring out the real nature of the maturing child. With each human being life begins anew. In this connection it is of the greatest importance that that life can unfold from within its deepest source. For a person to reach that source he must be detached from a strong focus on himself. Only then is it possible to give full attention to others, to things, and events. Here lies the beginning of his spiritual receptivity. His inner world will open up. He learns to see what a person can accomplish, what trustworthiness is, what the true order and the right disposition are.

This receptivity is not only of great importance for a person's growth to a mature life, but also valuable in itself, just as also the phase of childhood is valuable in itself. The child is just as much a human being as an adult. This theme recurs in Titus Brandsma's life. B. Meyer O. Carm., who followed his lectures, writes: "What the students especially appreciated in their professor was his understanding of everyone's peculiar bent and

ambition." The person who in his younger years is approached
in this fashion gains insight into his own possibilities. It strength-
ens his self-confidence.

In the breach for Jewish children

In the meantime, in his role as the president of the Association of
the Boards for the Administration of Roman Catholic Prepara-
tory, Higher, and Secondary Education (the VHMO), Titus
Brandsma was far from inactive. With the advent of the German
occupation Titus matured in his role as the coordinator of school
boards. Very soon an increasing number of common interests
emerged in education. On August 16, 1941, a decree came down
from the Department of Education to stop admitting Jewish children to secondary schools. These Jewish children who were already
enrolled in these schools might stay but must not be counted.
This last provision had a bearing, among other things, on the
extent of the government subsidy and the number of teachers to
be appointed.

National Socialism coveted space. It was a movement which
harshly removed countless people from their home and roots. They
collected them in spaces where they were hedged in by thick fences
of barbed wire; places of annihilation. Titus Brandsma, by contrast, aimed at giving people space, space in which they could be
shaped and develop and so become recognizable in society and
mean something. To Titus Brandsma this government measure
meant that young people were being deprived of the place where
they belonged, where they would find protection and their life
would unfold to its full significance. Now they were abandoned to
sheer meaningless caprice. Their days would lack all protection and
they would be nowhere.

As president of the VHMO Titus strongly objected to the above
measure. From the correspondence on this issue we learn that his
objections were threefold. In the first place he mentions the suffering inflicted within the Jewish community, the injustice done to
Jews. Second, there was the suffering inflicted in the schools.

In addition, there was the disruption of the school organization just days before the beginning of the new school year.

In the course of the afternoon of August 30, 1941, the Secretary General of the Department informed Titus by telephone that the Jewish children who had already been admitted could remain as pupils of the school and be counted as such. In a letter dated September 8, 1941, Titus wrote the school boards that he had expected that they themselves would have received notice of this from the Department. When this proved not to be the case, Titus himself took the initiative to inform the boards of this notice. He wrote: "After consultation with the higher leadership (the archbishop) and taking notice of the position adopted by (Protestant) Christians, I hereby inform you that we too must regard as a poignant act of injustice and a violation of the task of the church the fact that persons who have asked for the church's education are being violently withdrawn from it. The church, in the fulfillment of its mission, knows no distinction of gender, race, and nationality. We think, however, that with respect to pupils who ask for the education offered by Catholic schools we must distinguish two groups: those who do this for reasons of principle because they have become Catholic and desire a Catholic education. With respect to this group we must as firmly as possible take the position that we may not deny them admission to our schools. A second group is composed of those who, not being Catholic, ask for admission to Catholic schools for an incidental reason of a material nature. Here no principial reasons compel us to grant admission any more than principial reasons force us to deny it."

On September 18, 1941, after a telephone conversation with the Department in The Hague, Titus could inform the school boards that the recently issued rules pertaining to the nonadmission of Jewish children did not apply to children who received a basically Catholic education already before May 10, 1940, and can therefore remain at the schools for the VHMO and be admitted. Also in cases where there was no Jewish school in the neighborhood, Jewish children could still be placed in Catholic schools.

After that date the struggle to admit Jewish children continued with intensity. On October 7, 1941, Titus Brandsma sent a letter to all Roman Catholic schools under the VHMO. He wrote that he had received a written communication from the Secretary General of the Department in which the latter, having consulted with the German authorities, states that the interpretation of Titus Brandsma as conveyed in a letter dated September 30 is incorrect and that Jewish children may not be admitted to Catholic schools. "Exceptions to this rule, therefore, can no longer be granted." Titus continued his letter by again citing the Secretary General: "On the subject of exceptions in general there is ongoing consultation with the German authorities. From the insertion of the words 'naturally' and from the closing paragraph 'about the subject of exceptions in general there is ongoing consultation with the German authorities' I think I may conclude that there are nevertheless circumstances in which exceptions are made, or at least considered, and it may therefore be useful, especially for non-Catholic Jewish children who are asking for admission to our schools, to ask for permission via the mayor, as I advised in my letter of September 18." Titus Brandsma did not give up easily. He knew he was facing a superior adversary. A delaying tactic was his only means of resistance. In the final months of 1941, furthermore, he became involved in a fierce conflict with the Secretary General of the Department of Education over the government demand that clergymen and religious could not be directors or heads of a school. In a letter of December 29, 1941, to the governing board of the Catholic Teachers Association "St Bonaventure," Titus wrote: "In the present time, more than ever before, we must strive for conditions and relations which are in accord with our principles of justice, accommodation, and love." The German government was at this point paying increasing attention to Titus Brandsma and preparing measures to deal with him. The atmosphere was becoming angrier.

5. Journalism

It was in the spring of 1935, as Titus was making preparations for a trip to North America, when he found in his mail a letter from Cardinal J. de Jong. This letter introduced an incendiary new impulse into his highly mobile life and at the same time presaged a series of events he did not wish to avoid. He shoved aside a pile of papers on his desk: an unexpected letter from the archbishop deserved a bit of extra attention. The letter told him that the archbishop had appointed him to be the spiritual advisor of the Roman Catholic Association of Journalists. It took him by surprise. Would he be able to reserve enough time to perform his task well? At the same time he was immensely pleased with it. For a long time already the press and the work of journalists had greatly fascinated him. In Oss he had edited the local paper. In Nijmegen he had been linked as censor to the regional paper "De Gelderlander." This assignment from the archbishop suited him perfectly. When at the Carmelite training center by the Niagara Falls he was later giving conferences on the subject of Carmelite spirituality, he sought contact with the University of Washington professor who specialized in journalism, showing a readiness for the fray which is so decisive especially in the world of journalism.

On the 12th of May 1935, Titus was installed at Utrecht. In his word of thanks he said: "As Catholic journalists we must consistently keep in the foreground that which is positive and constructive. For us that is the only way – since it is the divinely willed way – to serve the Catholic cause. In the second place, we Catholic journalists must hold high the virtue of love. That too is the will of our good Lord. That love must come through in the tone we strike, the irenic tone of the Catholic press."[23] In saying these words

---

[23] B. Meyer, O. Carm., *Titus Brandsma*, Bussum 1951, 357.

Titus was not restricting himself to external qualities, the superficially correct; he was referring to an attitude which is rooted in the deeper feelings of the inner life. He mentions the irenic posture and respect for people. But he goes beyond that. We may not be satisfied with a universal human ideal with which virtually everyone can identify. Human activity changes in character. It is no longer focused on a purely abstract ideal but will from now on be bound up with a personal relationship. When we speak of the kingdom of God we mean the kingdom in which love for our human existence has been transformed into a personal relation with God.

The times were uncertain. Everything that happened in Germany was full of dark significance. In 1935, the year in which Titus joined the voices speaking in the world of the national press, the notorious Nuremberg Laws were enacted. Jews and other non-Aryans were excluded from citizenship. The free world was not capable of bringing the approaching violence to a stop. Titus's words about an irenic attitude and love and the will of God sounded otherworldly in that period. While people still hoped that the worst could be prevented, nobody knew how.

Titus soon felt at home in his new position. He regarded himself as a colleague amidst "his" journalists. The monthly magazine of this Association wrote that "Brandsma had a good sense of the interests of Catholic journalists."

After World War II J. Zwetsloot, writing about Titus Brandsma, commented: "… Journalism was attractive to him. He was fond of the press and the people of the press." Zwetsloot wondered if Titus was not describing himself when in just a couple of sentences he sketched the life of a journalist: "People speak of a hectic life. That is what the journalist has. There is no time left for himself."

It was not hard for Titus to picture the life of a journalist. Every year, from 1918 on, he wrote 104 articles about social and political topics in "De Stad Oss," a paper which he also served as editor. In addition he regularly wrote in "De Maasbode," "De Tijd," and "Ons Noorden." In "De Gelderlander" he had a regular column of his own. When he wrote that a journalist as a rule has little time left for himself, he was revealing something from his own experience. It was his own lot he was expressing in those words, his own daily experience and clashes with his own world. He was totally absorbed in his work without attempting to protect himself. Though he was a man of indomitable strength, as would become apparent from his advocacy of the freedom of the press, he did not know the art of playing for time when people laid claim on the few moments he had to spare. He was always prepared to do whatever presented itself, remained calm as he did it, did not look for excuses, and gave his attention without being pompous about it. Both characteristics suggest that he had a healthy measure of self-confidence.

A member of the board of the Society of Journalists wrote: "However numerous his activities were, for his journalists he always knew how to make time. To gain a proper legal position he did more than any board member. As an advisor and friend he helped numerous people. Many a time he managed to alleviate great distress, solving tragic cases of discrimination or dismissal through his intercession with management."

On the occasion of Titus's 40th anniversary as a member of a religious community, the president of this society wrote about the excessive demands people made on his time: "Out comes his pocket diary in which almost every day is booked full. But professor Brandsma knows the secret of 'elastic' days. They seem infinitely elastic, like his capacity and zest for work." It is the abundance of which there is constant mention in Scripture and which in the language of the Bible as also in the language of the medieval mystics is called the blessing of God. It does seem, however, as though the person producing this abundance is for all intents and purposes lost to himself. He has to refrain from ever demanding anything for himself and, if he did, he would experience how vulnerable his life had become. To have experience and inner contact with this "God of abundance" is unknown to people who know only the hard standard of utility and have a sharp eye for how they can take advantage of people and things. The mystical person continually lets go of himself. He in no way clings to himself; for that his reverence for life is too strong.

"He could take the lead even where he could not see where this would take him," wrote Dr. Joan Hemels in 1973 in an article printed in the periodical *Communicatio Socialis* on the significance of Titus Brandsma for the Catholic press.

Journalistic training

In those days "De Maasbode" and "De Tijd" were the best-known Catholic dailies. These papers were oriented to the Roman Catholic National party.

At the time that was considered a good thing. Besides the national press there was a well-developed regional press. The largest share of these papers were Catholic. Among them the biggest were "De Limburger Koerier" and "De Gelderlander." All together it was a fascinating business. In 1910, eight years after the founding of the Society of Catholic Journalists, there were twenty Catholic dailies. This number grew to thirty-eight in 1940 with a total of 471,800 subscribers, which at that time was one-fifth of the total number of daily paper subscribers.

In the daily press there was great diversity both as to geographic distribution and as to world view. It is clear that then we were still living before the days of the large conglomerates. The daily press underwent an enormous development. The society which the press reflected as a mirror was becoming more complex. Also in the business of daily papers technical developments and innovations succeeded each other in a rapid tempo. In such a situation staffers must be able to respond quickly and know the correct answer.

In the board meeting of September 12, 1936, Brandsma with great urgency brought up the matter of a training program for the journalists. He was aware that in the future increasingly heavier demands would be made on journalism. His proposal met with approval. A committee for journalist training was appointed. Titus Brandsma became the chairman and soon came up with an elaborate draft for a program. It was typical for him that in this plan for the training of journalists he described at great length the need for theory and practice to go hand-in-hand. Among other things he envisioned a plan of collaboration between the big dailies, field work and guidance by people from the world of journalism. He also believed that the training should be sponsored by both Catholic press associations: that of the directors as well as that of the journalists.

Recognizing both the commercial and the ideal aspects of the newspaper business, Titus had in mind a unity that is based on respect and makes it possible to gain insight into the values of the other. He writes: "A daily paper must be sustained by a single mindset which unites all the people who work there and this is best obtained by a training program which instills that mindset and, in the nature of the case, preserves the journalist from a fatal one-sidedness." This training course based on the "Brandsma plan" was discussed at a combined meeting of the boards of the two associations on April 7, 1938. A year later the secretary of the directors' association reported that no headway could be made. Thus, while the "Brandsma plan" had run aground, the idea that something had to be done remained alive.

In the same year the two associations appointed a commission to study "new forms of journalism," again under the chairmanship of Titus Brandsma. The problem which was to preoccupy the commission was the relation between the daily press and the new media. The radio, after all, was becoming increasingly important in the distribution of the news. This was unavoidable inasmuch as the radio was able to react quickly to whatever was happening in the land. Live coverage and commentary, moreover, is so fascinating that the paper is bound to lag far behind. But the radio was not the only rival. The weekly newsreel was fast coming into vogue. It ran regularly in the theaters while the daily press remained a world of words and included hardly any illustrations. The commission studying the consequences of this development understood that the idea should not be to defend one's own turf. The field is so vast, they reasoned, that there is room for many types of communication. The information industry has many aspects! A paper can confine itself to purely factual information; it can aim at shaping public opinion, or providing background information, and so forth. People should be able to find each other in a new form of cooperation in all these areas. The criterion for this cooperation, the commission believed, has to be technology: the technical possibilities of the different media must determine the role they play. Thus the daily paper, exploiting one of its own possibilities, can focus more on visual material like photos and graphics.

The legal status of the journalist

Events in those years succeeded each other rapidly. In May 1939 a commission was appointed to study the social and legal position of journalists. Again Titus was chosen as chairman, but this met with instant criticism. He gets himself too much involved in material interests, which is at variance with his function as spiritual advisor, said the directors. Titus, accordingly, stepped down as chairman, but remained active in the commission. The lost battle of barely a year before had not left even a trace of discouragement or hesitation in him. He openly, but calmly, stated his views. In the meantime these were well-known: it is his opinion that the independence of the individual should be respected.

To arrive at a collective labor agreement Titus composed guidelines and on April 16, 1940, from a hospital room on the *Prinsengracht,* wrote a letter containing a brief summary of a program. The directors of the Catholic dailies, however, remained totally aloof. In those years, accordingly, no collective labor contract was ever signed.

Titus saw that many people were not getting their due. They lived with dashed hopes, estranged from their real needs, driven by nameless powers which commanded them to pursue success and to be distrustful toward everyone. They hardly realized how tied down they were.

To Brandsma it was always very clear that what mattered was the independence of the individual. That was always his basic premise: that is something to which a person is entitled. It is a matter of justice. What we now describe as "formation for adulthood" or "personality development" Titus called independence or self-reliance.

In mental health circles people are accustomed to speaking of a person of a sound mind: someone who can bear the burdens of life, the burdens of his limitations, and his social obligations. Titus labored so that journalists and others could make independent judgments, were equipped to that end, and could see through sham and everything that is associated with it. That was his goal in the study of philosophy and that is also why he was a proponent of the study of philosophy in secondary education.

Conflict with the German authorities

Among Catholic journalists a strong consciousness-raising process had been set in motion. They had gained more influence, but the war put an end to that development. In general the managers of the daily papers were not forceful enough in their resistance to the oppressors. In that situation the occupying authorities found it relatively easy to control the Catholic press. Titus, for his part, entered upon the great struggle for the special responsibility of the press and freedom of speech. To him it was a matter of justice: the justice which had always been the core of Messianic expectation and which could never be completely codified. It took courage to enter this struggle. It is a courage which can drive a person to recklessness in the marginal area where violence becomes crafty and will harden itself. In this life-and-death struggle one often hears bellicose language which obligates no one to do anything. But Titus was not just a man of words: he did not sidestep the struggle which would ultimately demand of him everything a human has to offer.

In the final and exceptionally active period of his life Titus accepted the ultimate consequences of his many-sided involvement. He was active in many areas. People sometimes wondered whether he had not spread himself too thin. But while he had been able to divide his attention over numerous activities, he nevertheless continued to see clear lines of continuity and connection. In his thinking these lines always converged in the image he had of man. His ideal image was the person who is able to live and think independently and maturely and who has acquired so much respect for life and so much inner freedom that he is receptive to the hidden signs of God's presence in this world.

In this final period Titus was active in two areas: the pursuit of freedom in education and the pursuit of freedom of the press. In February 1941 the Department of Education decided that members of a religious community had to turn in 40 percent of their salary and could not exercise leadership functions. A vehement protest was submitted by the Catholic School Council and the Alliance of School Boards of which Titus was the president. By way of this Alliance a kind of united front was established. Repeatedly Titus traveled to The Hague to rescue what could be rescued. "In any case," he wrote, "they must know what we view as just." According to Dr. Jos de Boer, the secretary of the Catholic School Council, Brandsma was "the soul of resistance" when it came to education.

Toward the end of August 1941, all Jewish children were denied access to the schools. On behalf of the bishops Brandsma notified Catholic School Boards "... that the church will not make any distinction on the basis of gender, race, or nationality." Jewish children, accordingly, remained in Carmelite schools until, in a later stage of persecution, they too were struck by the public measures.

On December 18, 1941, the offices of the daily papers received from The Hague a telex message in which the Department of Public Information and Arts informed them that the Dutch press did not have license, on grounds of principle, to refuse advertising from the N.S.B. (the Dutch organization in league with the German occupation). In a conversation with the archbishop, Dr. Jan de Jong, the decision was made that Titus would send a letter to all the editorial boards of Catholic dailies in which he would make clear that the advertisements in question must not be placed. At the same time it was decided that Titus would visit all the Catholic dailies to explain this refusal to the directors and top editors and to receive from them a written statement of agreement.

He started this journey on New Year's day, 1942, a journey which lasted nine days and took him to all parts of the country.

In January the Ministry of Security made the following decision: "On the ground of the systematic preparation of a resistance movement aimed against the German occupation authorities, Pater Titus Brandsma must be immediately arrested and sent to a concentration camp." At the time Titus was in Merkelbeek and suspected what was in store for him: "Now I am getting what I rarely had and what I have always desired. Now I am going to a cell and will finally become a true Carmelite!" He used this image of a cell at moments in his life in which, perhaps in great inner conflict and solitude, something began to occur in him which was decisive for him. By this image he was referring to that other reality in which a reverse order obtains. A cell locks a man in on all sides and leaves him alone, for a long time, a time of bitterness without consolation. But for Titus a cell was a place where the hours no longer hold sway over a person, where there is timeless silence, and where God's world totally envelops him. When he exists in that other world, he views the hard events of life in that light and hence sees everything differently. It is the focus of a mystic who in his mind's eye sees another order. When he spoke about that reality he was speaking about the experience of joy which always stayed with him, also in the dark days that lay ahead. In these words of Titus we hear echoes of the tension which always exists between the contemplative and the active life, a tension which keeps everything alive and continually compels us to raise questions.

On Sunday, January 18, the last day which Titus Brandsma spent in freedom, he traveled to Oldenzaal. He had assumed the responsibility for an Armenian boy whose parents had fled the Turkish terror. He came to ask how things stood and whether anything needed to be arranged. The same day he also traveled to Utrecht and Amsterdam where he spent the night and where the following day he celebrated mass in the St. Boniface church – for the last time. That day, Monday January 19, he traveled to The Hague where he had a conversation at the Department of Education. The next day, Tuesday, January 20, he was to return to that city, but this time as a prisoner.

6. The Arrest

On Monday afternoon January 19, 1942, there were two persons at the door of the Carmelite monastery on the Doddendaal who wanted to speak with professor Brandsma. One of them was an agent of the German Gestapo. "Steffen is my name," he said by way of introducing himself. "On orders of the commander-in-chief of the security police and the ministry of security I must, professor doctor Brandsma, temporarily take you into protective custody. At six thirty we are leaving for Arnhem and tomorrow we will go on from there. I would like to search your room immediately. Would you please show us your room, professor?"

Throughout Europe this dreaded and relentless order was given. No questions were asked; there was no need for respect, or time to say goodbye or anything human. Everywhere this lethal work continued. Millions were fetched with a revolver in their back and never returned.

Titus Brandsma's life, a life that was full of movement and activity, had suddenly been interrupted. His intimates had urged him to leave Nijmegen and to think of a place where the Nazis would be unable to find him. At the same time they knew how driven Titus was and were not surprised to find that he could not easily decide to withdraw from the battle and to await the end of the war in some lonely attic room.

From this time on he was a prisoner, and completely delivered up to dark forces. Titus was immediately aware of what this meant. He said to his prior – who had, in the meantime and uninvited, joined the remarkable company – that there was a document on his desk which required some haste and asked whether the prior would speedily mail it. The prior was given to understand that such a thing could not be permitted under the new regime. Titus Brandsma's study was sealed. His role was over. It must have struck him as painful that he was confronted with obsessive power in this way and that he was eliminated without mercy. This violent world was utterly foreign to him. As a man of reflection he always had high respect for life. It had not escaped his neighbor across the street, Mr. 't Hullenaar, that a couple of German policemen had rung the doorbell of the Carmelite monastery and that nothing good was to be expected. He kept a close eye on the gate.

When the gate finally opened, he saw Titus coming out, a small thin figure between two robust Gestapo agents dressed in imposing uniforms. The prior stood in the gate, motionless, a defeated man. He briefly waved – a helpless gesture. Titus did not see it.

A car stood ready. A loud bang signaled that a door was being slammed shut. The silence which followed seemed more intense than usual. The Doddendaal Street once more became peaceful.

Life not only assumes a stable form as a result of the road we have chosen and the values we have sought in freedom. It is also shaped by what we encounter on that road and what has unintentionally gained a hold on us and in connection with which we sometimes wonder in desperation what we must do with it. Our paths are frequently crossed by fate. A fatal illness, or a car accident, can send our life spinning in a different direction. Fate is a remote incalculable agency which can suddenly so disturb our life that our calculations no longer add up and our dearest expectations are dashed. Before that fate we are powerless. It can neither be justified nor does it have any mercy. Fate works as a blind force that respects nothing and nobody. We can experience fate in many ways and try to learn to live with it. Titus knew very well what limitations mean. Several times he had to interrupt his work on account of illness. He believed, however, that by a conscious acceptance of the resulting limitations we can nevertheless generate great efforts to achieve our goals.

Some years before Titus had led a spiritual retreat whose motto was: "The enclosed garden." On the first page of his text he had drawn a sketch of it: a garden completely enclosed by walls. This image served as his starting point as he described the process of spiritual growth and formation. He used the metaphor to make clear, among other things, how we must let ourselves be instructed and shaped by symbols which confer a deeper, hidden, meaning on the limits every human has to contend with. Only in this way can we come to a good understanding of the laws of life and the incalculable counterforces of life. Titus described full of wonder how when the sweet pea goes its own mindless way this climbing plant goes nowhere. But when the gardener guides it and attaches it to the garden wall, it can blossom beautifully; that is, our strength lies in letting ourselves be guided.

In the religious life we are dealing with forces which, while seeming to be opposed to each other, can be very fruitful if they achieve a subtle equilibrium. We are speaking of the balance between a sense of independence and being called within a given set of limitations which are unavoidable. From within the perspective of the religious life Titus knew the struggle to achieve this balance. He also knew that the moment we lose it we can no longer be happy. The crucial question now was whether in this violent situation he had enough inner strength to preserve this vital balance.

Scheveningen

The former penitentiary on the Van Alkemadelaan in Scheveningen, also called the "Orange hotel" in honor of the many prisoners who had been arrested because they resisted the German occupation, now became Titus's place of residence. Now, sitting by himself in the silence of cell 577, he was acutely aware how odd it was to take the days as they came. He speaks about it in his accustomed light vein. "It is really something," he wrote on January 23, 1942, "to still end up in jail at the age of sixty." A week later he wrote: "Certainly, when you are thus brought into a jail cell, late in the evening, and the door is shut behind you with bars, locks, and keys, you do for a moment feel a strange sensation. True, the humorous side of the case that in my old age I still managed to end up in a jail cell tended to make me laugh more than that the tragic side of it could depress me: still, it was strange. There I was. I arrived rather late, at least by prison standards, about 7:30 p.m.

By then it is bedtime and the work is done. No one counted on me anymore. No cell was really made ready for me; on the other hand, there is not much to be made ready. I was given a jar of water, a towel and, additionally, a cloth to clean things up with or as a napkin – who knows. Somebody had called to say that I still had to eat, so I did get a roll that also had to serve for the following morning, plus a tin cup with skim milk. On the table stood a tin cup with water; a straw mattress lay on the bed and there were two blankets. I had better make the most of it. Although in other cells the light went out at eight, in my cell the light was left on a half hour longer".[24]

The interrogation

In the first week of his stay in Scheveningen Titus was brought to The Hague to be interrogated by the Germans on the subject of undesirable activities. "Tomorrow at 9 a.m., bring in professor Brandsma from Nijmegen for questioning!"[25] Wednesday morning at 8:30 the prison van drove up to take him to the central office of the Ministry of Security *(Sicherheitsdienst)*. The interrogation took place at the Binnenhof, room 137, the press division, where Herr Hardegen, Hauptscharführer, ("chief division leader") was in charge. There Titus was given a chair to sit across from a representative of a movement which wanted once and for all to wipe out the disgrace and events of the past and which now tried to appropriate for itself the image of the master race.

The interrogation was focused on the purpose of the trips Titus Brandsma made with stops at the editorial offices of the Catholic daily press.

Hardegen asked precise questions, questions entirely expressive of the mentality of those in power.

In this interrogation Hardegen looked for evidence that the Dutch bishops were aiming to strengthen their own position of

---

[24] *Mijn cel,* Bergman, Tilburg 1943.
[25] Idem, 396.

power. Titus did not respond to that angle. His answers were short, nuanced, and rooted in his love of truth. For him the truth transcends all human interests and is all-embracing.

The search for truth gives a human being dignity. Titus Brandsma was basically a philosopher. It was his field, the discipline in which he had been schooled. The most characteristic attitude of a philosopher is that he wants to understand what he sees. he wants to separate appearance from reality. He does not want to be misled by external impressions. He is, therefore, always in search of truth and keeps asking himself how he can find it. The Nazis had a view of truth that was entirely their own. They had taken a specific aspect of social reality and chosen it as their standard of truth. Their answer was: "Wahrheit ist was dem Volk nützt" ("The truth is what benefits the nation"). In so doing they had deprived the truth of its certainty. The truth was no longer separate from the interests a given group was pursuing. Given their thesis the interest of their own nation became the norm for what had to be considered the truth for life. With that the truth was delivered up to caprice and dependent on political interests. The philosopher knows that truth is independent and must be sought for its own sake.

The German party men appealed to an ideology. The application of it was imposed on the people and controlled by the army and the police. The Nazi system left no room for any personal conviction. A Nazi official represented a totalitarian system. His foremost belief was that individual freedom led to chaos. That being the case, the power of the state was bound to increase. In addition there was the phenomenon of depersonalization: many allowed themselves to be swept along by the display of power. The authority of the Nazi was derived from his position in the party and not rooted in his personality.

Hardegen had carefully prepared himself to conduct a thorough but business-like interrogation. To Hardegen's question what purpose his trips served when he visited the editors of the Catholic dailies, Titus's answer was a firm rejection. The editors had to be orally informed that the limit of the permissible had been reached and that the editors must from now on put up resistance on grounds of principle. In the interrogation Brandsma did not avoid confrontation. He did not "feel out" his opponent. He frankly stated where the boundary lay and further elucidated this point candidly in the ensuing conversation. He left concern for his personal safety far behind him and did not sidestep the danger. It happens more or less frequently that, when they stand face-to-face with danger, people especially demonstrate amazing courage. Danger challenges them. In the face of danger it becomes crystal-clear where they stand. Without realizing it, they show how much resistance they can offer.

A serene confidence and even boldness comes through in Titus's defense. At the end of his reply to the question why he had done what he did, Brandsma stated that the bishop had charged him to do it but that it was also his own conviction that drove him. This was an obedience that surpasses ethics. In the first few sentences of his reply Titus Brandsma identified himself with the patrimony of his fatherland. In him one hears the voice of a people who will never give up the right to live in freedom. Titus summed up the things he had always asserted. It is a conviction which is evident in his attitude and makes his explanation clear.

The literal text of the interrogation has by chance been preserved. It was discovered by a member of the resistance movement, Hilbrink of Zenderen, because the Germans, during their hasty departure on May 1945, had to leave the dossiers behind.

> *Hardegen:* What was the purpose of your travels when you visited the editorial offices of the Catholic dailies?
>
> *Brandsma:* The editors had to be informed orally that the limit of the permissible had been reached and that the editors must from now on put up resistance on principial grounds. A further purpose was to acquaint ourselves with the objections and sentiments of the Catholic editors. Additionally it was our intent that the bishops would draw their conclusions from these findings.
>
> *Hardegen:* Was your intent, in taking these trips, to gain a precise picture of every editor in particular?
>
> *Brandsma:* That was not my intent, for even a negative attitude would not have altered the position of the Catholic Church in this

case. I did, however, request that the predominant majority of the Catholic editors would declare their solidarity with the attitude of the bishops.

Hardegen: Is it the case that the editors who wavered had to be firmed up and possibly won back for the Catholic principles?

Brandsma: On this point, too, I can answer that I did not think of this directly, although this has been the result of the influence exerted on them.

Hardegen: Did the editors have to be put under pressure vis-à-vis the wishes of the bishops?

Brandsma: From the side of the church it was emphasized that the editors, in case they should make propaganda for the ideology of the N.S.B. (National Socialistic Movement), they would incur the penalties that have in the mean time become known. Archbishop de Jong also expressed this consideration in his letter. During the negotiations a number of editors pointed out the danger that they would run financial risks. When the Catholic Church stands up to defend Catholic principles, it first of all considers the ideal side of the issue and only indirectly the material loss that may result for believers from compliance with the precepts of the church. In my opinion, the ideal position was decisive also for the majority of the Catholic editors. The Catholic church is strong and powerful as a result of the unshakable firmness of its religion. At all times there have been people who, if necessary, gave their lives for the church as martyrs. The Dutch episcopacy is convinced that Catholics, when they all pull together, constitute an enormous source of political strength. In this time of uncertainty their faith gives the members of the Catholic Church the strength they need to make large material sacrifices.

Hardegen: Is it the case, then, that since this disposition of its believers is known to it, the church is determined to sabotage the decisions of the occupying power or of the Dutch authorities, in order in this way to endanger the internal peace of the country and to prevent the national-socialistic worldview from gaining acceptance among the Dutch people?

Brandsma: The Catholic Church in The Netherlands adheres to the ordinances of the occupying power or of the Dutch authorities insofar as they are consonant with the principles of the Catholic Church. When there are fundamental objections against such compliance, the Catholic Church refuses its cooperation, and accepts all the consequences which may arise from this refusal.

Should this attitude and the resulting actions seriously endanger the internal political unity of the country, then the Church deeply regrets this, but does not feel responsible for it. It opposes the world of national socialistic ideas on grounds which are anchored in its own worldview and its religious convictions. In my opinion it is deplorable that the occupying power promotes the ideology of the N.S.B., because the Dutch people and the Dutch clergy in particular want nothing to do with the N.S.B. leaders. The Catholic Church considers it incumbent upon itself to strengthen the attitude of all the Catholic functionaries who occupy a leading position.

Hardegen: Why did not the archbishop or the Roman Catholic Society of Journalists do everything in its power – before proceeding to influence the people – to first give them a chance to express themselves orally, as this in fact happened subsequently?

Brandsma: It was not our intent to influence the people of the press; it was rather our plan to gain an idea of the general mindset of these people. We were aware that with respect to this question there already was a common attitude. On the other hand, we hoped we would make more headway with the Government Commissioner if people did not only have to judge by expectations but could in fact point to clearly marked positions. In conclusion, I want to repeat that the Catholic Church will only observe the decrees of the occupying power and of the Dutch organs of state insofar as they are compatible with the basic principles of the Catholic Church. In the event that the authorities should undertake measures which are not consistent with Catholic doctrine, the Church will be forced to reject and ignore such measures.

I have been informed that I must remain in custody until this matter has been further cleared up. I am making the attitude of the Dutch Episcopate my own.

The Apologia

On the third day of his stay in cell 577 Titus Brandsma was instructed to submit a written explanation of why the Dutch people, and especially the Catholic segment of the population, are opposed to the National Socialistic Movement (N.S.B.).

His resistance to this movement, after all, is the occasion for his arrest. Before this arrest he was making his round trip visiting the executive offices of the Catholic Daily press. Acting on instructions from the archbishohp J. de Jong he discussed with the directors the refusal to accept the advertisements of the N.S.B. on grounds of principle.

In this defense Titus Brandsma first of all observes that National Socialism originated in Germany to prevent an economic collapse. In a later stage it became increasingly materialistic and anti-religious. The N.S.B., however, sought to transfer this movement to The Netherlands, not for economic reasons but on ideal grounds. Titus Brandsma then describes the historical development of the Dutch and demonstrates that the N.S.B. movement does not link up with that development.

In the second place, writes Titus Brandsma, the Dutch nation is opposed to the N.S.B., because its members are highly incompetent and unfit to give leadership. "Incompetent" in the sense that they have no natural aptitude for governing and "unfit" in the sense that they have not been trained for administrative posts. His language is becoming more vehement. He felt the great distance which existed between him and the false game played by these schemers. His judgment is now harsh and merciless.

In the third place, according to Titus Brandsma, there is a psychological reason for the repudiation of the N.S.B. Inasmuch as this movement was unable to implement its program it enlisted the help of Germany, a greater power. This violates people's sense of national dignity. Titus ends this *apologia* with words from the world in which he is at home. It is a prayer. He makes no attempt to define what, in his opinion, has to be done. It is not an indictment, but a prayer for reconciliation with the God who transcends everything and who will give us what now seems unattainable.

God bless The Netherlands,
God bless Germany,
God grant that both peoples
may soon stand side by side,
in peace and freedom,

in acknowledging him and for his glory,
for the well-being and prosperity
of these two so closely-related peoples.

In this *apologia* Titus Brandsma, accordingly, describes three characteristics of the N.S.B. which make clear why the Dutch people as a whole repudiated it. First, the antinational character of this movement. Second, its lack of competence to give leadership. Third, the inner weakness of the movement. He, on the other hand, speaks from the perspective of the foundations of society, justice and freedom, and opposes these to the rule of violence.

Still another aspect of the inner freedom out of which these words were written came to the fore in this piece. Titus rose above the situation in which he found himself. He left behind his feelings of annoyance and anger. He described independently how he thought about matters, but was at the same time totally focused on the truth. He could not write any other way. He *lived* in the truth. He was bound to the inviolable laws of life. It was precisely when he did this that he was totally himself. When he ended this piece, laid down his pen, and once more went over the text as a whole, he must have felt himself to be the university instructor. The piece is objective, yet sharp. The repudiation is clear. The conciliatory words at the end were characteristic of him. He is completely recognizable in these words.

The words he wrote down and the feelings he expressed in them are in complete agreement with his deepest convictions. He could speak his mind unhindered and was in no way a prisoner. Titus Brandsma wrote this in freedom, but his concept of freedom differed totally from that of the Nazi officer at whose bidding he wrote his defense. The Nazi officer abstracted freedom from the reality which has its own laws. Titus witnessed to an experience of freedom without falsifying it by the prejudice or ignorance which turns freedom into arbitrariness.

7. "I am happy in my cell..."

When Titus was told after the interrogation by Hardegen that his custody would be extended to obtain further clarification from him, it became clear to him that his stay in prison would last longer than he had thought and that freedom was a long way off. On the one hand, he was conscious that during his imprisonment he could not count on any fairness and that his future looked frightening. On the other hand, he was still the person he was in the monastery on the Doddendaal street in Nijmegen. At first he was still protected by the aftereffects of his connections with life there. These aftereffects, however, declined rapidly. What frightened him was that national socialism had left behind the basis of human life and plunged into pure arbitrariness. Nazidom revealed the inhumane human, man's dark side, guided by the desire to be absolute lord and master over himself and the world.

Over against this self-idolizing man who with his world stood alone, Titus witnessed to the person who believes in the living God of revelation. He did not passively await whatever would be further done with him. He refused to be daunted and did what many have done in a "hopeless" situation: they establish order in the small piece of life still left to them. Titus did this in his own way. He did not look for support and comfort in the past, or in the many ways in which he had made himself useful to others; instead in his own little world he put things in their place and gave a special meaning to the space in which he lived and to the time still left to him. He sat down at the shabby little table, took a piece of paper, and wrote down the words *cella continuata dulcescit*, a beautiful statement from the *Imitation of Christ* of Thomas à Kempis. It means: "A cell becomes sweeter to the degree it is more faithfully inhabited." With these words Titus detached himself inwardly from the grip which the Nazis had on him and turned his disadvantage into an advantage. These words about faithfully inhabiting one's cell have uniquely helped many to become conscious of their inner strength.

In the case of radical changes what matters are the inner possibilities. We cannot feel at home in a new situation overnight especially when the change is sudden and undesirable. The human mind has to be made fit. It must be made fit to let go of its sense of security and to be able to accept the unfamiliar. A monk knows this experience. He has become familiar with the silence of his cell. This space becomes congenial to him. Now his mind is able to open up. He accepts a new – not self-chosen – security. He is astonished, gives in. In the silence of his inner room the monk learns to listen inwardly. He gains a deeper sense of his own self and of his responsibility. A more mature consciousness develops in him.

When Titus gave the slip of paper with his beloved text a place which he could readily see, he looked at it with approval and with a smile considered how full of trust his motto sounded in this strange environment. However long it might last, he wanted his stay in Scheveningen to reflect the theme of this text from Thomas à Kempis. At the same time he could not help realizing that a very heavy time lay ahead and wanted to prepare his mind for that as well. He took a second piece of paper and wrote on it a brief text from John of the Cross: *pati et contemni*: "to suffer and be despised."

When Titus describes how in his cell in Scheveningen he arranged for a place of prayer, our minds involuntarily leap to the familiar medieval religious mini-paintings. These small wooden panels were made with a great love for detail. They are childlike, authentic, intimate, and full of tenderness. The minutely sketched details immediately capture our attention. With almost childlike ingenuity Titus pinned little prints and texts on a checkerboard. They are precious symbols which reinforce the experience of a perceptible nearness. In his memory he rediscovered his own monastic cell. In prison he is now in the place where he belongs. The recollection was deeply meaningful to him, because these images which were so precious to him helped him accept the suffering he experienced. By identifying himself with these images he tried to find his way amidst the bitter experiences of the present. Directly in front of him he beheld Christ on the Cross and in his mind celebrated the Eucharist. He prayed the canonical hours and felt united with his fellow brothers – perhaps with a greater intensity than in better times.

When we read the letters Titus wrote from prison, we immediately realize that here a person is speaking to us who had a realistic view of his situation and was always prepared to see the hopeful side of it. Sensitivity to what is hopeful, however, usually also carries with it sensitivity to suffering. On that subject Titus only very seldom said anything. The piece of paper on which were written those few dark words about suffering makes clear that suffering was a reality for Titus, a reality which occupied him with the realization that suffering would bring him closer to God. The words are radical and hard to understand. What can be their meaning? They can only be spoken by those who had tasted a sublime form of the experience of God. They remain enigmatic for those who do not know the experience. It is the pain which divests a person of everything that makes him unfit to be touched by that love. It is a pain which always remains because our human shortcomings and life's contradictions always make themselves felt. Herman Andriessen puts it very sharply: "Those who do not experience their wounds cannot arrive at true spirituality."[26]

Much has been written about the mental changes of people who have been locked in a prison for a long time. Clouds floating past barred windows or confused sounds coming from the street can suddenly disconcert prisoners. Everything that happens to them now feels different. In a time of imprisonment, what is joy? And what is grief? If the prisoner is as nearly as possible to remain sane, i.e. to remain himself, he will have to order his life anew. He will have to give his days another meaning. If he succeeds, he will find a different freedom, one that is totally inward.

[26] H. Andriessen, *Spiritualiteit als modern* verhaal, Titus Brandsma lezing, Titus Brandsma Instituut, Nijmegen 1994.

In the death camps there have repeatedly been people who wrote about their loneliness and their tortures. Why?

S. Dresden observes that "there are various reasons one can advance for this: the writer wants to air his feelings or tries in this manner to make clear to himself the situation in which he finds himself. It is his intention to somehow hold onto what has happened to him during these years."[27]

There exists a very diverse literature of resistance. At the time our country lived under the breath of a very evil spirit. We can still catch the indignation over this fact in the poetry of resistance. The poems of that time, despite their lack of poetic refinement, often have an impassioned quality. They were recorded on the fringes of human existence, in darkness and great despair, as a plea for freedom and respect for human dignity. Many poems of that time remain anonymous. The poet was not important. It is even a question whether those who wrote these texts actually wanted to be poets. Shocked by events, they did not want to perish in silence. They wanted to appropriate again the things that had been taken from them by violence and they could only do this in rebellious, bitter, and hopeful words. They wrote because, despite their appalling experiences, they held onto the inviolable values of existence. They testified to a strong will to live. Those who survived the camps could not remain silent; they had to tell the world about the indescribable things they had witnessed and experienced. They did this to warn: it could, after all, happen again. Or they wanted to free themselves from the psychological consequences. Those who amidst the horrors of the camps found the strength to write down something sought, by writing about them, to escape those horrors. They wanted to get past them, to experience contact with the world of the living. Even in the present they wanted to create distance. In the camps they were nothing and nobody – they were going to die in solitude without leaving a trace of their existence. What certainty would they still ever find in the remainder of their life?

---

[27] S. Dresden, *De literaire getuige,* Raster 57, Amsterdam 1992, 14.

Titus Brandsma freed himself from the desolation of imprisonment by making a secret covenant with his cell. Others, by contrast, freed themselves by breaking out of their cell into the inner world of their imagination and by returning to their own small world.

> The writing prisoner transports himself into the presence of us all and even when he cannot get past the barbed wire, by writing he breaks through his hermetic enclosure. He rises above it, even better, he denies his being closed up, his being nothing and nobody.[28]

In the literature of the camps the question keeps being raised whether the camp experience can be conveyed to others. Those who survived the death camps were aware that this was hardly possible. Still they felt a strong need to write down their story and to search for words to reveal something of the immense suffering they witnessed. Primo Levi says:

> We can perhaps ask ourselves if it is necessary or good to retain any memory of this exceptional human state. To this question we feel that we have to reply in the affirmative. We are in fact convinced that no human experience is without meaning or unworthy of analysis, and that fundamental values, even if they are not positive, can be deduced from this particular world which we are describing…. We do not believe in the most obvious and facile deduction: that man is fundamentally brutal, egoistic and stupid in his conduct once the veneer of civilization is peeled off, and that the *Häftling* (prisoner) is consequently nothing but a man without inhibitions. We believe, rather, that the only conclusion to be drawn is that in the face of driving necessity and physical deprivation many social habits and instincts are reduced to silence.[29]

In the letters of Titus Brandsma one will not find any realistic descriptions of the suffering, no condemnations, not a word about retribution or punishment. He is rather inclined to forgiveness.

---

[28] Idem, 15.

[29] Primo Levi, *Survival in Auschwitz, The Nazi Assault on Humanity*, London 1976, 79 [slightly modified to conform to the Dutch – Tr.].

He has detached himself from the facts. That is not the same as ignoring them. It is a way of liberation. That is what he wants to witness to. The mood in which his letters originated must have been a mixture of anxiety and longing for attention and protection, but he does not record these feelings. But they do come through, even though his language is rather conventional. In his poems and letters he wanted to witness to another world in which other, hopeful, forces of life hold sway. The core of what he wanted to witness to openly was the imperishable dimension in humans which points to the mystery of God. Titus did not rack his brains about the question of the fairness or unfairness of the facts. "Take the days as they come, the good with a grateful heart, and the bad for the sake of those which follow, because misfortune is only a passerby." He called this "my favorite saying" and had written down the French text on a slip of paper: *Prenez les jours comme ils arrivent….*

The way in which Titus reacted to his imprisonment is characteristic of people with a strong will to live. He did not allow himself to be overpowered by the space in which he was locked up. Coolly and searchingly he describes his cell so that it loses its threatening character. It is a disarming description of what he finds there:

> The little cell itself is not unseemly; it is long and narrow with at the end, over its whole width, a bed. This defines the width of the cell which must be 1.80 to 1.90 meters, six times the length of this sheet of paper plus a small piece at the bottom (down to the little arrow). The length is about double the width, twelve times this sheet of paper plus a small piece at the bottom (down to the arrow below). The height is about the same as the length. The side walls have been built in fine masonry for two-thirds of the length. I count 65 bricks upward plus a rather wide joint; the wall around the bed has been covered with concrete which is cleaner. To the height of the door the walls are painted a pale yellow; above that level they are white. They look fairly clean. The door in the center of the front wall has been stained brown on the inside. In the middle of the door there is a square iron hatch through which the food is passed. Above it there is also a tiny peephole trimmed with iron which up until now, however, I have not seen opened.

The first evening I thought there was no window, but the next day I noticed that it had been installed high above the door abutting the ceiling over the entire width of the cell in three sections. The middle one can be easily opened with a lever. The light is therefore abundant and the possibility of ventilation very good. But the little windows show me little else than the air; now and then a seagull skims past. Till now, for the largest part of the day, the windows have been covered with the most beautiful flower scenes, but the sun and the heating system see to it that now and then, at least here and there, some spots of light appear. Yes, there is a heating system. Above the bed, at the height of a couple of meters, three heating pipes run through the room. They do not produce a lot of heat. On the coldest days I shiver a bit all day long, but at least the cold is reduced a bit and quite bearable. At least, even though I am sitting still, it is not cold enough for me to put my coat on.

The floor is made up of rather large blue floor tiles but in front of the door lies a good little mat which I put under the table during the day and in front of my bed at night. "Table," I must say, is a rather grandiose word for it. It is a small drop-leaf table on the left wall, somewhat smaller than the spread-out daily newspaper I use as the tablecloth. I cover my little table with the "Vaderland," which shows its splendid name on both sides. In such a bare cell something, certainly, has to show. I do not have a chair, only a stool, a tripod, which however does not sit badly. When I need something a bit more comfortable (a person gets more tired here from doing nothing that at home from working hard), I put my stool close to the wall next to the table and so have the easiest armchair. There is not much to tell about the remaining household effects. It can be summed up quickly: a dustpan and a brush to keep my cell neat, a small pail and a mop, a little wastebasket, a larger pail with a toilet seat which can be closed tightly and is taken out once a day, and a water jar of blue stone. Finally a small zinc soap dish and a hat rack with three hooks. The electric light has been attached to the wall directly above the folding table. It is turned on and off from outside the room."

Titus here explores his cell with the eye of a camera. He does not try to penetrate the inner reality of the cell but meticulously describes the exterior. As a result this small space has nothing in it that is threatening. He accepts the cell and himself as the prisoner in that cell. He forces himself to look at it, unaffected by fear or fury. As a result everything about him remains itself and [his] respect for these things and the secret of their existence is preserved.

Intimacy of the Cell

Solzhenitzyn, in his book, *The Gulag Archipelago*, describes a similar experience. With awesome sensitivity he writes about the cell in which he spent eleven years as a political prisoner.

> All your life you will remember it with an emotion that you otherwise experience only in remembering your first love. And those people, who shared with you the floor and air of that stone cubicle during those days when you rethought your entire life, will from time to time be recollected by you as members of your own family. [...] What you experience in your first [...] cell parallels nothing in your entire *previous* life or your whole *subsequent* life.[30]

The intimacy, the silence of a monastic cell, where it seems time stands still, is actually an archaic image in our culture. The plain lines, the white walls which catch the pale light take away all heaviness and fill the space with an intimate silence which produces the realization that there exists an inner order which assigns to all things their proper place. In his first letter to his parents from Boxmeer Titus wrote: "I am very happy in my cell." The silence of the monastic cell which embraced him gave him a profound peace which filled him with the sense that God was near. In this silence he felt at home. After Titus had lived in this monastery for some months he wrote about the first impressions he had gained in this world, a world entirely new to him. He described his cell, and the things he found there, with meticulous attention to detail. He could have written about numerous impressions, about the severe facade of the building, or about the beautiful light in the cloister. He restricted himself, however, to a description of his

---

[30] Aleksander Solzhenitsyn, *The Gulag Archipelago*, New York, I-II, 1973, 180.

little cell, the most quiet and intimate space of the monastery. It was the space where, in silence, he would learn to understand the voice which called him and which would lead him nobody knows where.

When Teresa of Avila wrote about the inner life, she used the image of the castle of the soul. There are many rooms there. The room that is located in the center of the castle is the image of the most inward part of a person, the core of his/her personality. Titus, too, wrote about the room which belongs to the center of the building. He entered into a relation with his cell, a lasting relation. From this point on, it played a role in his life. His cell, like every other monastic cell, looked very plain. Every day again its simplicity, its intimate light and silence, remind the monk of the deeper reality he is in search of, the reality he wants to live for. His cell became a symbol of his inner culture, of the indisturbable serenity of his life's core. Titus could be "in his cell" everywhere. The boundaries are relative. When he prayed and when he worked on his texts, all sense of boundedness disappeared. The space in which he lived opened up and became a spiritual space.

Titus Brandsma often spoke about inwardness. He was familiar with it. He spoke about it with a certain warmth, sometimes even with tenderness, as though he was aware that it concerned something that was precious and at the same time very fragile. In the retreat he had developed around the theme of "the enclosed garden" he wrote that we must plant "inwardness" as the first flower in the garden of our heart.

To "stay in one's cell" means to seek out the silence, to be by yourself. In the silence and the gentle interior light attention for one's own inner self awakens and grows. The cell is an image of self-reflection. Many, however, do not know the road to one's "inside." It means withdrawing from the circle of people, from the pleasure of conversation, from what fascinates, disturbs, and confuses a person.

Titus Brandsma lives in his own inner world. This world is not a separate world which exists in isolation from daily life. His inner world materialized where he lived, amidst his fellow brothers, and the many others with whom he had his contacts. This "being by himself" occurred in the peace and silence of the deepest core of his life where he experienced the intimacy and power of God's nearness. But it is also realized in the threatening situation in which he now finds himself. He allows himself to be filled to the full with this silence – also in the prison cell. In one of the first letters from his prison cell in Scheveningen he writes: "*Beata solitudo* (Blessed solitude!). I am altogether at home in this tiny cell. Though I am there alone, our good Lord was never closer to me than he is now." One gets a picture of somebody who, though in prison, extends the line of his life with a firm hand. In this situation he does not change; he simply remains himself. So also in a prison cell he is in his familiar home. His cell will always be there; it exists as a symbol both at the beginning and at the end of his life. It continues to enclose his life and is the unshaken symbol, not of confinement, but of inwardness.

Often people like Titus are consciously with God; they continually seek him. They thirst for the imperishable; they seek the things that cannot be destroyed. They seek this in their inner life and increasingly have the sense that then they are in their own true space. In the silence of their inner life they know that God is close to them. In him they experience the imperishable goodness of life. It is the silence which continues to do its work so that God can be found also in the active life, even where events are sometimes wildly capricious.

Titus has not told us much about himself. He kept his feelings hidden in the intimacy of his inner world. Even in the greatest desolation Titus could be happy. He was by himself, hence really at home. This sense of joy was independent from everything that took place around him. That joy was so strong that nothing from without could hurt him. The camp guards could not reach that inner world.

In Scheveningen Titus said that he was happy. He was alone. The door of his cell was barred. He had been abandoned to caprice. Everything seemed contrary to his well-being. How could a person be happy here? Nothing is more mysterious than the lot of people who live from an interior source of strength. When in such a situation they speak about happiness they are not talking about a superficial, immediate, ready-made happiness. Camus says: "Heroism does not mean a great deal; to be consistently happy is much more difficult."

We are speaking here of a joy that nobody can take away. This joy does not depend on good or bad days. It is not an obvious thing. It is not clear where this joy comes from. One can experience an upsurge of joy that has a clear source. When Titus was a boy in Friesland and at dawn saw the early light of the sun spread over the green pastures of the broad Frisian countryside, he must have felt a wave of happiness. It was the joy that comes to a person from without and can be very deep. But when he writes in Scheveningen that he is happy he knows that that joy comes from within, from the depths of his inner life. No one can take it from him nor is it something we can just appropriate at a moment's notice. We cannot receive it as a matter of course whenever we please. It transcends us; it cannot be reached in one's own strength. The roots of it lie in the unshaken conviction that life is imbued with values which are holy and imperishable. It is that experience which has given many people the vital inner strength to keep going. The values with which their will-to-live is imbued are extratemporal and therefore cannot be affected by time. No violent actions can in any way change that. After all, we are talking about values which we have not created ourselves. There is an even deeper reason. The believer acknowledges God as the fountainhead of the inviolable values of life. For Titus God was the ground of his existence.

By staying in a cell, monks gained an unusual experience. Their lifestyle may seem a flight from the realities of life; in reality, in their isolation they take themselves along with all their emotions, their longings and restlessness. In their cell they are confronted with themselves and discover that it takes courage to remain in a cell alone with themselves. Those who had the courage not to run from themselves experienced that their mind opened up to the truth of their own life. They remained true to their cell and discovered the riches of the inner world. They found a deep peace and became ever more conscious of living before the face of God. The cell gave them a broader sense of reality. They learned to look in the familiar for what till then was unfamiliar to them. Their stay in a cell made them initiates in great secrets.

The cell also had a special meaning for Etty Hillesum (1914-1943), a young Jewish woman who died in Auschwitz. For her the cell was a symbol of protection, a place to which one can withdraw. The "high walls" protected her from the confusion and menace of the merciless life she experienced around her. The cell spoke especially to her imagination as a space for prayer, a place where she could be with God. It was the place in which she wanted to stay, the space which surrounded her in whatever appalling situation she might find herself. In her diary, on May 18, 1942, she wrote the following:

> The threats from without are becoming ever more serious; the terror is mounting by the day. I am drawing prayer around me like a dark protective wall. In prayer I withdraw as into a monastic cell and then again step outside: stronger and more "collected." For me this withdrawal into the closed cell of prayer is becoming ever more important and also necessary. This inner concentration builds up high walls around me, walls within which I find myself again and, out of all the distractions, gather myself up into a single whole. I could imagine there will be times in which for days on end I lay on my knees until at last I felt that protective walls came to stand around me, walls within which I could not fall apart, and lose myself, and die.[31]

Anwar Sadat, the president of Egypt who was assassinated in 1981, when he spent a long time in prison, found the way inward in his own fashion. Like so many others, he experienced how this way always leads to greater depth and how, by that liberation process, he ultimately discovered his deepest and most real "self":

---

[31] *Etty, de nagelaten geschriften van Etty Hillseum,* 1941-1943, Amsterdam 1986, 380.

It was four o'clock in the afternoon when I found myself inside Cell 54. I looked around. It was a completely bare cell – except for a palm-fiber mat on the macadamized floor, hardly big enough for a man to sleep on. (...) For eighteen months I lived in that cell, unable to read or write or listen to the radio. (...) One of the things Cell 54 taught me was to value that inner success which alone maintains one's inward equilibrium and helps a man to be true to himself. No man can be honest with others unless he is true to himself (...). Inside Cell 54, as my material needs grew increasingly less, the ties which had bound me to the material world began to be severed, one after another. My soul, having jettisoned its earthly freight, was freed and so took off like a bird soaring into space, into the furthest regions of existence, into infinity. (...) Once released from the narrow confines of the "self," with its mundane suffering and petty emotions, a man will have stepped into a new, undiscovered world which is vaster and richer. His soul would enjoy absolute freedom, uniting with existence in its entirety, transcending time and space (...). In that period I was initiated into that new world of self-abnegation which enabled my soul to merge into all other beings, to expand and establish communion with the Lord of all Being. This could never have happened if I had not had such solitude as enabled me to recognize my real self. (...) It was genuinely a conquest, for in that world I came to experience friendship with God, the only friend who never lets you down or abandons you.[32]

Sadat realized in his cell that he was completely dependent on his own resources. He did not look outside of himself for something that could free him from fear and a sense of abandonment. Letting go of everything that could possibly give him support from without made it possible for him to turn completely inward. In that way he became conscious of the depths of the "self." Once he was freed from the confinement of his own "self" he experienced the space of the cell differently. The constriction of the bare cell and the moist walls which enclosed him evaporated. He entered a world

[32] Anwar el-Sadat, *In Search of Identity, an autobiography,* New York 1977, 67-93.

unknown to him. He experienced something of the total existence which transcends time and space.

Sadat in the end, when he describes his experience of God, speaks a very intimate language. He had experienced the friendship of God, the only friend who never abandons a person. Here he touches the core of religious desire. He had found the source. He had passed through fear and darkness. There was no other way. There was no other desire that brought everything together in this life. For Sadat it was a time of renewal and of entering into an undiscovered world. "This could never have happened if I had not had such solitude as enabled me to recognize my real self." Sadat did not neglect to say where he learned to know the deep significance of the interior way: "One of the things Cell 54 taught me…" Sadat's experience links up with an ancient wisdom which the desert monks discussed a lot. A brother asked the old monk Moses to give him a word that could help him. The old man said to him: "Go, sit down quickly in your cell. Your cell will teach you everything."

This account of three people who were violently robbed of their freedom, though they came out of very different traditions (the Catholic, the Jewish, and the Islamic tradition), display strong kinship with each other. This profound kinship between the experiences of the Carmelite, the Jew, and the Muslim, is not accidental. It can also be found in the many stories, testimonies and symbols of these religions. Carmelite spirituality can be viewed as a bridge between Judaism and Islam. There also exists a common source. It is the great inspiration of the prophet Elijah which is of eminent significance for all three: Carmelite spirituality, Judaism, and Islam. Its deepest ground is the search for the living God.

The experience of time

When Titus was given the assignment to write an *apologia,* he asked for his little pipe and tobacco, and in addition got his own watch back. It had stopped. In his cell-notes he wrote: "Now I have my

own time, regardless of Greenwich, Amsterdam, or Berlin."
For Titus time in prison was not just the time he had to serve.
In his first letter which he wrote from his cell in Scheveningen he
described how he spent his day. He drew up a schedule which gave
him the sensible rhythm of prayer, labor, and rest: "After my
evening meal I pray the Angelus, observe the Adoration in spirit
with the monastery, light a cigar, and take my little evening walk,
three meters up and three meters down and so on, back and forth,
just as in the morning. At six o'clock I again start writing a bit
until shortly before eight. Then I make my bed and pray my
evening prayer in front of my bed. For the rest it does not bother
me much that the light goes out. I continue to pray a bit longer
and then tuck myself in till morning." For him time was not a
stream which uninterruptedly continued to flow and to which one
simply had to submit. He did something with it; were he not to
do so, time would do something with him.

The stories of people who managed to put up resistance against
the arbitrariness of the injustices and the hopelessness of the imprisonment often strongly resemble each other. They had been shocked
in the depths of their existence. When they write about this they
touch upon feelings which are deeply rooted in human existence
and are true of everyone. Those who survived the concentration
camp tell us how by losing their sense of time they increasingly lost
their grip on life as well. Sam Dresden wrote: "The former inhabitants of the camp say they had no idea of time. The only thing
they knew was that it was night."[33] These people felt they were
helplessly dragged along by time. Before they were imprisoned, the
hours of the day had their own rhythm as hours of work and exer-
tion, hours of rest and relaxation, hours of encountering others
and hours of silence and being by themselves. But now there was
no structured sense of time. When time flows on without meaning, life cannot be maintained. They were dragged along by time
to a horrible end.

---

[33] S. Dresden, De literaire getuige, Raster 57, Amsterdam 1992, 82.

Titus Brandsma writes that at fixed times he prayed the prayers of the hours. They were the same hours as those in which his fellow brothers in the Doddenzaal monastery came together in prayer. It is the morning prayer when light dawns; the noontime prayer when the sun reaches its zenith; and again in the evening when the sun sets and disappears. It is a divinely-sanctioned marking of time which gives to the praying person an inner structure or order. Prayer shaped him in the direction of an inner discipline. He lived in a cosmic rhythm which made him sensitive to measure and balance, the eternal cycle which, coming and going, always again returns to itself. The beauty of this rigorous order was part of Titus's life. He was known as a person who had all the time in the world for a store clerk who had lost his job. People who dropped in on him to talk about their failures and frustrations got the impression that he had nothing else to do but listen to them. It is remarkable that he kept this proper balance even when he had come into a world where evil was in the saddle.

8. Living in God's Presence

In the early days of his imprisonment Titus forcefully stated his position vis-à-vis the Germans. During his interrogation he assured the Gestapo officer: "In the event that the authorities should undertake measures which are not consistent with Catholic doctrine, the Church will be forced to reject and ignore such measures" and "The NSB [the Dutch Nazi Party] is at odds with the realism of the Dutch people. It is even more violently at odds with the religious disposition of the population. It has totally misconstrued the very strong Christian character of the nation." Coming through in these statements is the voice of a man's basic conscience. It is characteristic for a person who has been shaped through and through by this voice that the statements he makes are well-considered and formulated rapidly. His clear-sighted businesslike attitude remains alert and consistent. He does not sink away in vague complaints. Both during his interrogation and in his defense, he clearly mentions the terrifying consequence of his attitude. During his interrogation he said: "The Catholic church is strong and powerful as a result of the unshakable tenacity of its religion. There have always been people who, if necessary, gave up their lives as martyrs for the church." In the statement of his defense: "From their history Catholics know countless martyrs who were exemplary in their willingness, if necessary, to offer up even their life for the confession of their faith." On both occasions he mentioned martyrdom, not out of panic but governed by a reliable intuition. Titus would not shrink from the extreme consequence of his conduct.

Finally, the strength of his attitude came through in a poem, a poem with which he struck the theme of his imprisonment and in which he expressed himself very personally about accepting his lot. In the poem he speaks of the source from which he draws the

strength for that acceptance and accepts the fearful road that clearly
lay ahead. The poem is a dialogue. Acceptance tends especially to
come about in dialogue. In this poem – which soon after his death
became very popular – he tells how at a crucial moment of his life
he learned to acquiesce in the suffering which would inevitably be
his lot. If we want to judge the poem at its true value, we must read
it as a prayer. The words of praying people are frequently moving
when what comes through in them is powerlessness and emptiness
on the one hand and a deep desire to somehow reach the ears of
the God who is silent.

> O Jesus, when I look on you
> My love for you becomes more true.
> And yours, I know, will never end:
> You see me as a special friend.
> This calls for courage on my part
> But pain is a blessing for my heart,
> For pain makes me become like you
> And leads me to your kingdom, too.
> I feel true blessing in my pain;
> Such suffering for me is gain,   —
> For what your providence will do
> Is make me one, my God, with you.
> Just leave me in this cold alone
> Although it chills me to the bone.
> No visitors, no one to see
> To be alone is good for me.
> For you, Lord Jesus, are right here;
> I never felt you quite so near.
> Stay with me, with me, Jesus sweet,
> Your presence makes my joy complete.
>
> (Translation by Henrietta Ten Harmsel)

Contemplative Attention

In the first stanza of the poem he speaks of love – experienced
as grace – as purely a gift, something we can never have at our
disposal no matter how hard we try.

O Jesus, when I look on you
My love for you becomes more true.
And yours, I know, will never end:
You see me as a special friend.

Titus, removing a small print from his breviary, put it on the narrow ledge that served as his table and placed it against the whitewashed wall so that he could clearly see it. He got down on his knees and looked at the face of Jesus on the print.

He was totally turned inward. Something came alive in him which, like the sudden appearance of a clear light, dispelled all confusion and uncertainty. Entering a depth that is unfathomable, he felt himself being absorbed into the sacred. He knew the pure breath in which that which is essential opens up. He again became aware how strong the love of God had grown in him.

My love for you becomes more true.

This had not always been so strongly present in him, for there was also a time of not-seeing, of not-understanding, a time of emptiness and dread. The words "more true" recalls what had happened to him in the last few days: the arrest which abruptly ended a life that was full of plans and expectations, ended it forever, his room having been sealed. Fairness and goodness had vanished. Evil, with its enigmatic face, dominated. His inner silence had been disturbed. Everything suddenly stagnated. He felt darkness descending on him and the deception that was shamelessly present everywhere. He needed time to adjust to it. Now, before the face of his Lord, his cell no longer enclosed him and no longer held him captive. Light, unveiled light, had returned. His cell has now become a place of quiet encounter. For that reason he immediately adds:

And yours, I know, will never end.

The poem has become a dialogue! Peace – as well as acceptance and hope – returned. He returned to himself and to him who sustained his life. This was the spring from which he drew life: the consciousness that he was loved by God.

In 1931 he had written: "… that the mystical life is an abundance of God's love and grace, an abundance so rich that God's indwelling and working in us speaks clearly, and we are completely filled by it." Over the years this love had deepened and grown in strength, rooted as it was in this source. But now its strength was being put to the test.

Deep within him Titus had heard the invitation to come out of himself and to take steps toward the other in trust. It is an art that has to be learned step-by-step. We have to relinquish the idea that we are the center of the world, that people and events exist to serve the fulfillment of our needs and desires. When we renounce this expectation, the true value of the world again becomes visible. We discover a depth that is both mysterious and fascinating. The most marvelous aspect of this attitude of disinterestedness is that God, who is concealed, will reveal his face. It comes home to us that he is not far from us.

The word "you" is present in every line of the first stanza. From his childhood on Titus had lived in this "I-thou" relation to his God and now he came back to this experience. In this dialogue he experienced wonder, emotion, fear, and gratitude. As a result of the word "friend," with which the stanza ends, these four lines achieve an air of great intimacy. Perhaps, concealed behind this word "friend," there is a kind of nostalgia for the Middle Ages, for courtliness and almost childlike piety such as he saw and admired in ancient texts. He calls himself a "special friend." He experiences the love of God as an election, for this creative love endows him with incomparable unicity. He knows that this applies to every person and he therefore always displayed great attentiveness to simple people. He was not deceived by status and respect but had an eye for the person behind every facade. The emotion of "friendship" is a striking element in the poem. It comes back in the "presence" mentioned in the last stanza. A true friend is close to us, thinks of us, and sides with us. In each other's presence we experience intimate contact with and recognition of the essential character of the other as a gift.

Suffering as the Face of God

Nevertheless the appeal to friendship sounds like a cry of distress, for in those dark days Titus Brandsma learned to know dread, a deadly chill, and the grinning face of abandonment. What will the end be like? Now that much in life had lost its value, Titus sought support in what he had deeply experienced in the past and has true value in the present.

> This calls for courage on my part
> But pain is a blessing for my heart,
> For pain makes me become like you
> And leads me to your kingdom, too.

Titus Brandsma sought his strength in the inner life. He witnessed how people for whom political power and riches are the supreme good get trapped in inhuman structures. They are imprisoned in things which are transient and unstable. For them, therefore, to lose the war was to lose everything that was desirable. Since they were so deeply entrenched in that conviction they often reacted cynically. Titus, willy-nilly, found himself in that world, their prisoner, delivered up to their capriciousness. This was not easy for him and it demanded from him more stamina for suffering than he had expected. Although it can be read as a complaint, there is an almost sad resignation in the second stanza: "Oh, well, really all pain is agreeable to me." When we fall into the hands of violence which knows no mercy, we have to regain our confidence.

Titus attuned his life to the voice that spoke from within him. Never again did he let go of it, for it was stronger than all the other things that moved him. "In the depths of our being we come upon the activity of God by which he sustains us and we are led and guided by him. We have to go to its deepest source to re-discover ourselves in God."[34] This voice does not prompt him to rebel against the suffering inflicted on him, now that the chips are really down. He remains true to the insights he cherished in 1934: "Allow

[34] Titus Brandsma, "Evangelische Peerle." De Gelderlander 7-5, 1939.

me to start with something that to some sounds negative: resignation in time of suffering and disasters. I know there are people who
consider the message of resignation obsolete, who would much
sooner preach resistance and rebellion than resignation, but the
truth is we live in a world in which suffering is unavoidable, in
which suffering on account of our own sins and shortcomings has
no meaning. It is a denial of the true state of affairs if we do not
prepare for something we cannot escape. While for a moment it
may seem a sign of strength if we do *not* tolerate suffering and
rebel against it, we can only respect and venerate those who endure
suffering with true valor, a spirit of sacrifice, and love. The world
would look very different if rebellious cries were no longer heard,
complaining stopped, and suffering was viewed as Christ taught the
disciples of Emmaus to see it. This is not to say that all suffering
on earth should be perpetuated. Love would alleviate and remove
more suffering than rebellion and resistance could ever banish from
the world. I wonder if the world of our day does not have the most
urgent need for men and women who have the courage, spirit of
sacrifice, and love to bear the suffering of this time. Who still val-
idates, with passionate love and courage to die, the words of our
good Lord when he said, as he did, that 'his yoke is easy and his
burden light'?"[35]

Titus, rather than being despondent now that he himself was
struck by this dreadful fate, in all quietness rises above his suffering. Suffering is real: blind, tyrannical, and absurd. Many cannot
see why it should be so. They can only see the confusing and
destructive effects of it. Suffering for them is an approaching
disaster, an overpowering event to which they are not equal. This
so disturbs them that they look for all kinds of rationales that
might serve as explanation. They want to protect themselves from
suffering and banish it from this world. All attempts, however, fail

---

[35] Speech delivered 4-2-1934 on the occasion of the Roman Catholic student
society's foundation day celebration. In: B. Borchert, *Mystical life*, an anthology,
Nijmegen 1985, 210-221.

miserably. Dread and resistance continue to pursue them. Suffering is part of the vulnerable human condition; it enters the fabric of everyone's life.

Mystics have similarly experienced suffering as something that comes upon them uninvited and that has power over them. Suffering has some kind of "intentionality." Mystics believe that suffering has a positive meaning, even though it turns against us and seems completely meaningless and absurd. They have respect for the whole of human reality and, being realists, they do not withdraw into some kind of childish dream. Destruction and death is part of human life, a life that is not self-caused. In all of reality they search for the Face of God which reveals itself even in places or situations where we, in self-will, deny it access. But since mystics are also people, "holy indifference" is the best way to form a friendship with insurmountable suffering.

Great mystics have therefore always viewed suffering as a way to become transformed in God, a means of breaking down our resistance with a view to delivering ourselves up to the incomprehensible reality of God's creative love. In this love-encounter with God we discover within ourselves forces of which we were previously unaware. Thus human logic breaks down and we begin to see suffering as a source of power and hope.

In submitting to this concrete form of suffering, Titus Brandsma discovered how it brought him much closer to Jesus. Unintentionally, the likeness with the Man of Sorrows grew in him:

> For pain makes me become like you
> And leads me to your kingdom, too.

Now Titus himself has to go down the mystical path in its most extreme implications. There was nothing to escape or prevent here. He knew the archbishop's assignment was dangerous. People had warned him that he was being sought and would be wise to go underground. For him, however, there could be no compromise: the Catholic press could never place itself at the service of a system that denied the dignity of man.

Let my Soul be a Shroud

Faithful to the truth about man, Titus accepted the way he inex-
orably had to go. Without any reservation, he put his own life on
the line. Freed from attachment to self-preservation he worked for
the liberation of man. Transformed in God by suffering his consciousness became unified. The whole poem bespeaks the correct
ordering of his values.

> I feel true blessing in my pain;
> Such suffering for me is gain,
> For what your providence will do
> Is make me one, my God, with you.

This third stanza is central in the poem. Its words well up from
the praying man's inmost. Is it even possible to be "happy" in a jail
cell? Is not this a pious illusion, a wish rather than a reality?
We find the source of this experience of happiness in the first
stanza: "... Your love, I know, will never end."

Titus Brandsma did not merely experience the insane world in
which he landed as all-powerful. Amidst all the violence, he
encountered another, an inviolable reality: the love of God. It is
only religious experience that opens our eyes to this dimension.
In the midst of all the pain and suffering he remained deeply
conscious that God was there for him and loved him. Thus he
lived in the awareness that his life was rooted in God, not in
himself.

While the ground sank beneath his feet he found a foothold in
the hidden depths of his existence. This realization gave him an
inner peace that was inalienable. Whatever happened, God was
closer to him than he was to himself. In this central core external
suffering could not touch him. For Titus this was not a temporary
emergency solution for this extremely threatening situation, since
this realization was also the sustaining power of his existence in
earlier years.

On Passion Sunday, 1921, when he lived in Oss, he wrote the
following prophetic words: "Let my soul be a shroud in which the

people put you to rest. May the image of the Lord put its imprint also on it so that I will always remember how Jesus loves me." This realization brings about a change in perspective which turns one's values upside down. Suffering is no longer suffering. A fate that knows no justice and goodness loses its meaninglessness and in an incomprehensible way turns into divine election. Is this possible for a human being? No, for this experience is solely based on the foolishness of divine love.

This fate undoubtedly remains hard. Dachau, the camp for which he was headed, remained a scene of horror. Still everything changes if he accepts his fate as "a traveler to your kingdom," a sign of intimacy with the love of God.

By his surrender to God the sense of his fate changes. In the manner in which he bears his fate the love of God becomes visible. To be happy in a graceless world is counter-intuitive. The happiness of which Titus speaks is of a different order. It has its origin in the conviction that his life is rooted in God and that God is close to him – even intimately close. This is his conviction, a conviction which strongly matured even amidst the privations of a death camp.

The Mystical Space of Solitude

He lived through this life in all its darkness and cruelty to the full. This unbreakable force remained active in him right up to the disconsolate end.

> Just leave me in this cold alone
> Although it chills me to the bone.
> No visitors, no one to see
> To be alone is good for me.

In all his life Titus Brandsma had been a very busy man. It may surprise the reader that now, in his jail cell, he says: "Just leave me in this cold alone, although it chills me to the bone."

Total concentration on God's presence absorbs all his powers. Having arrived at this point in his life, Titus realized that only they can love who give themselves away without protecting themselves and who persevere in this in solitary faithfulness. We shrink from this when it occurs at the cost of our own life. In desperation we then withdraw into the closed world of our own "self." It is therefore hard for us to glimpse the painful transformation to which Titus is called and the fascinating freedom this brings him. He ends up in a solitude in which he remains faithful to God with undiminished intensity. Disregarding his instinct for self-preservation, he finds it bearable to say: "Just leave me in this cold alone, although it chills me to the bone."

Many people experience being alone as a bitter hardship in life. In contrast, Titus Brandsma calls solitude "the very choicest lot." Solitude, for him as a Carmelite, was a space filled with meaning, because there he discovered the hidden meaning of suffering and being alone. Silence and solitude took him into the space of his own heart. Familiar with silence he was all by himself, undivided, all his attention fixed on the one essential to which he knows himself called. Within the clear plain walls, in the intimate light of his cell, he finds the inner silence and refined attention which makes him sensitive to the friendly presence of God. As a result of this intimate state of concentration his life becomes ever more inward. Wherever he is – in a crowded train compartment, in the practical atmosphere of a business meeting, amidst noise or boredom, he is always in the inner silence of his cell. All that penetrates there acquires a pure sound. Silence and solitude, after all, refine and reinforce the sense of what is essential, as well as the power and vitality of it.

Increasingly Titus Brandsma became the Carmelite the Carmelite rule envisages: a person who "stays in his cell" because this is the space in which the deeper and mysterious dimension of life ever-increasingly penetrates the human consciousness. His familiar saying "Cella continuata dulcescit" ("A cell becomes sweeter to the degree it is more faithfully inhabited"] gradually gained a very particular meaning now that it concerned a *jail* cell.

I never felt you quite so near

As a contemplative he encountered the God who exerts his influence on all the layers of one's existence. His Carmelite life is the fruit of the way of silence and solitude amid community.

> For you, Lord Jesus, are right here;
> I never felt you quite so near.
> Stay with me, with me, Jesus sweet,
> Your presence makes my joy complete.

The bare walls of his jail cell, the relentless jingling bunch of keys of the jail guard, solitary footsteps in the hallway – it all boiled down to the repeated experience of abandonment, an abandonment full of chill and unrest. Many inmates became panicky and looked for a way of escape. A yellowed little print from his Book of Hours, placed against the drab wall of his cell, helped Titus return to his own world. God is near. In his life his relation to God was marked by nearness. Titus said of himself that he was born an optimist. He is most familiar with the God of the seventh day who saw that everything was good. God, after all, sees what is invisible, incomprehensible, and unattainable: the deepest layers of a person and his ultimate lovability. God sees the deeper areas of inaccessibility and tells us they are good because they are loved by him. Titus's image of God was one of inner depth. For him God was not a cool and distant light but a loving face and intimate nearness.

However contradictory this may seem, his days in the jail cell in Scheveningen were filled with this sense. He entered the prison with a smile. The truth is: he did not view his situation as tragic. He even saw the humor of it.

> O yes – when, late in the evening, you are led into the cell of a prison, and the door is closed behind you with bolts and locks, you do for a moment have a strange feeling. The 'humoristic' element of the case, the fact that in my old age I ended up in a jail cell, tended more to make me laugh than that the tragedy of it could depress me, but – I confess – it did feel strange. There you stand all of a sudden.

We see God when we allow ourselves to be transformed in his infinite silence. If we do not allow this inner silence to shape our inmost being, we remain blind to the subtle signs of God's presence.

The intense experience of Jesus' nearness was not confined to a few moments of undisturbed happiness. From deep within himself Titus Brandsma asked to be left alone in all quietness ("No visitors, please") for over a period of many years he had practiced silence as a way of life. Focused on his inner life as he was, he picked up the barely perceivable signals of the passing of the Hidden One. Externally with empty hands, he now sensed more than ever the constant presence of him in whose fullness he sought rest. Just this extremity was enough for him.

> *Beata solitudo* (Blessed solitude!). I am altogether at home in this tiny cell. As of now I have not yet been bored in it. On the contrary: I am alone here, O yes, but our good Lord was never closer to me than now." "I can cry out with joy over the fact that he once more allowed me to completely find him, although I cannot be in touch with people and people cannot get in touch with me. He is my only refuge and I feel safe and happy. I am prepared to stay here forever if he so wills it. I have seldom been more happy and content than I am now.

At the beginning of his *via dolorosa,* the road that was to take him to Dachau and inevitable death, Titus Brandsma wrote down the incomprehensible words: "I never felt you quite so near" and "never was our good Lord closer to me than now." To our ears it sounds bizarre and inhuman that he should express such intense happiness in this situation. Yet his assurance of Jesus' nearness is wafer-thin like the "prayer": "Stay with me, Jesus sweet, your presence makes my joy complete."

It is an experience which lies completely outside of our power. We cannot apply ourselves to the acquisition of this divine nearness. We can neither cause, nor hold onto, the experience of God's nearness. God himself takes the initiative for this encounter: "Once again he has allowed me to find him altogether."

This nearness is of a completely different order from that of people. The person who has allowed himself to be found by God sinks into a solitude which, as extreme abandonment, humanly speaking, is very painful, yet filled with intense divine joy: "Although I cannot be in touch with people and people cannot be in touch with me," yet "your presence makes up for everything; I feel safe and happy. I want to stay here always."

The person who has lost all human comforts and has his back to the wall becomes fully receptive to the sense of God's nearness. We regard the unexpected as a gift; it falls into our lap, as it were, and is not something we can demand. It is grace. These unexpected elements give us a sense that life is a gift. If we link the first with the last stanza, we read that Titus Brandsma first of all directed himself to the Other, his God. In every line the word "you" occurs. This produces a strong feeling of nearness, a feeling which is expressly stated in the final stanza. If God is near to us, that is only because of his love. This basic thought serves as the framework of the poem. In this context words like "lonesomeness," "suffering," "being happy," acquire a new meaning, a meaning which has little or nothing to do with human emotionality. This is characteristic for the mystic, a man who gives expression to this fundamental shift in perspective in paradoxical language. In this way Titus Brandsma invites us, too, to enter into this prayer of acceptance:

> Your presence makes my joy complete.

After writing down the text of this poem, Titus rose from his little "desk." He needed to detach himself for a moment from a set of concentrated feelings which deeply touched him as he wrote the words down. He now took his little walk, as he himself describes it:

> I do not walk far. Three meters one way, then three meters back, pacing up and down, over and over. Often I pray as I walk back and forth until, tired of my stroll, I sit down on my stool by the table with my back resting against the wall....

He thought at some length about the statement he had written down in black and white and about its consequences. These are things worth suffering for. There is not a word he would take back.

He had been instructed to write this document, and had to do it. The poem is a witness to his most sacred feelings: this is where I stand; this is who I am.

For Titus, seated in front of his primitive desk in prison, the hours glide by in silence. Everything is different here. No appointments. No time pressures. No hurry. Even nightfall feels different from what it was like in his monastic cell at home. Against the wall, on his little table, he could read his favorite text from Teresa of Avila:

> Let nothing disturb you; let nothing alarm you. All things pass, only God never changes. Patience conquers all. Those who hold onto God lack nothing.

Now what should he do? Perhaps he then harked back to one of the limitations of his former life. Since he had been involved in numerous, quite divergent, activities, it was inevitable that important things would suffer neglect. Writing a book about the life of Teresa of Avila was one of the great projects he never got around to doing. He even had an agreement with Spectrum Publishers in Utrecht, where Teresa of Avila's biography would be published. He recalled the early years in the life of the monastery when he compiled a small anthology of her works. In 1924 he had translated some of her mystical works. So now he was going to work at that project. There were problems, however. He had no sources at his disposal, nor did he have enough writing paper. But he was not going to give up because of these limitations. This time he was going to succeed. He did not want to postpone the project any longer. So he took Cyril Verschaeve's book about the life of Jesus that lay on his table and proceeded to write his own text in the margins and in the limited space between the lines. In the midst of his busy former life he could only have written this book in between many other activities. Now he was still looking for space and finally found it between the printed lines of an existing narrative.

In this way he was able to work on the story of Teresa for a month and a half. Seven chapters were completed, though he had wanted twelve. The text ends on page 273 of Cyril Verschaeve's book. On the morning he wrote that page, the door of his cell was unbolted. It was Thursday, March 12. Someone walked in:

> On instructions from the superior commander of the security police and the security ministry I must, professor doctor Brandsma, invite you to come with me immediately. We are going to Amersfoort. The van is already parked out in front.

9. Good Friday in Amersfoort

Wartime had its much dreaded acronyms: NAZI, NSB, SS, SD, PDA. PDA is the acronym which stands for the notorious police transit camp at Amersfoort *(Polizeiliches Durchgangslager Amersfoort)*. In August 1941 this former training camp of the Dutch army was rebuilt into a concentration camp. To get to it the prisoners had to walk from the railroad yard through the city and through residential neighborhoods to the camp that was located on the Appelweg.

> Visible in the windows, above and below, of most residences and behind closed lace curtains, were numerous silhouettes, especially those of children. Usually the silhouettes did not move. Sometimes, feebly and furtively, they waved. Children who waved were very quickly pulled back. It was a farewell from the inhabited world – now a realm of shades.[36]

Once they arrived at the camp, all the prisoners were given the same reception.

> First you entered the 'rose garden.' That was a permanent feature. You did not know how long you had to stand there – sometimes it lasted a whole day. It was called 'the rose garden' because it was surrounded by barbed wire…. You had to hand over your possessions, undress, and receive your prison outfit: two wooden shoes, two rags to wrap around your feet, a pair of pants and a coat. You were given a number (Titus's number was 58), which was attached to your pants and your coat and then you were sent to a block.[37]

During this long wait in the "rose garden," a piece of land surrounded by barbed wire and located behind a barrack, Titus's

[36] F. Bakels, *Nacht und Nebel,* Amsterdam 1977, 56.
[37] Sporen van de oorlog, 1989, 100.

thoughts must have drifted to the image of "the enclosed garden."
In that lecture he had referred to the rose as "the second flower
to be planted in our garden, the flower par excellence, the rose,
symbol of love. Our garden must be a rose garden." But he also
saw before his mind's eye Jesus, "crowned with thorns to be King
of Love. For us, too, the rose has thorns, very sharp ones sometimes."

In camp "Amersfoort" Titus met people who had been struck
by misfortune in a totally unexpected way. The people who
were driven together in the transit camp did not know what
awaited them. For the Security Ministry this uncertainty was
a fearsome means of weakening the morale of their opponents
and so of controlling them. For the prisoners it was sheer
torment.

When they sought their bunk in the evening and, curled up
under a gray blanket, found a bit of rest, live images of domestic
security promptly sprang up in their mind. Soon, however, these
images had to make way for the specter of a firing squad or the horrors of a concentration camp. There was no justice, no mercy, no
trust. They had been delivered up to unpredictable forces. Their
fate was inescapable.

The prisoners who were sick lay in barrack 4. Every morning
Titus went by the bunks where the sick and exhausted lay to talk
with them. Almost every day someone died. Titus, semi-healed of
dysentery, took care of Jan Hoffmann, a young man from
Scheveningen. Outside the barrack Titus found a couple of
heavy stones, which he rinsed off and heated on the stove in
the middle of the ward. Using them in the place of hot water bot-
tles, he leaned them against the sore areas of the young man's
body. But it did not help. It was more his presence that for a
moment alleviated the suffering: the hidden power of his presence, unemphatic, and devoid of too much concern for his own
suffering.

Words can hardly add anything to the power which radiates
from one who lives from within a circle of inviolable inner freedom. Survivors of Amersfoort said later that they were impressed

by the "quiet, deep nature of this devout Catholic." Dr. Ronge
says:

> I myself am Lutheran but I have to say that in my life I have seldom
> had dealings with people who so strongly impressed me as father
> Titus Brandsma. There were people in Amersfoort of all sorts of class
> and standing but pater Brandsma knew how to win them all as
> friends. He was cordial to everyone, made himself available to every-
> one, also to people who disagreed with his convictions, even to com-
> munists. He was above all impressive by virtue of his spiritual invi-
> olability. I sensed immediately that I was dealing with a person who
> in ordinary life must have stood head and shoulders above the rank
> and file.[38]

In this scene of desolation the prisoners of barrack 2, lying in their
bunks in the evening, heard a few encouraging words from Titus
Brandsma. He walked past every bunk. He offered a hand to all
the men and with his thumb drew the sign of the cross on their
hand. In the darkness of their suffering they recognized this sign
as a symbol of suffering and of ultimate victory. The half-dozen
words he whispered to everyone came from a world of inner serenity. It gave them the strength to find themselves again. They had
a need for a word based on deeper values, for suffering and ultimately death as such have no meaning of their own.

A few of them felt steps had to be taken to make it a joint experience. By coming together they could reinforce the experience and
preserve it to counteract everything that was trying to destroy them.

> The Rev. De Geus and I had organized a small group of prisoners
> who felt the need for a short daily prayer meeting. Titus Brandsma,
> a professor of the Roman Catholic University at Nijmegen, held a
> series of lectures on a well-known preacher, Father Brugman – a very
> worthwhile project! It was passion week, so we agreed that every
> evening we would present a short meditation on the seven words
> from the cross.[39]

---

[38] B. Meyer, o. Carm., *Titus Brandsma*, Bussum 1951, 466.
[39] J. Overduin, *Faith and Victory in Dachau*, St. Catharines 1978, 75.

Dutch passion mysticism

It was proposed that on Good Friday Titus Brandsma, speaking for the prisoners of barracks 2 and 3, would present a meditation on suffering, precisely on the day of Holy Week when the believing world memorializes in silence the suffering and death of Christ. The prisoners knew that this had to be done very cautiously since the Nazis were fearful of all forms of religious fellowship.

The title for Titus's lecture was: "The significance of Geert Grote in our spiritual literature. The unique character of Dutch passion mysticism." He spoke about Dutch literary history as a cover for his meditation on the religious meaning of the mysticism of suffering. This meditation began as a lecture. He told his audience about his own experience. One senses the continual communication existing between his activities as a scholar and his religious life. It was his final lecture. The text of his presentation as he wrote it down is a brief and concise summary. Toward the end sentences made way for just some detached words.

It is certain that during his meditation Titus gradually departed from his text. It was forbidden, after all, to speak about religious matters. "If the camp leadership were to get a hold of his paper, they should not be able to find anything in it that was forbidden" (statement by Th. van Mierlo, April 15, 1943, Titus Brandsma files). The fascination of his speech would have been due especially to the manner in which he told his story. It had the genuine ring of what he himself had experienced. This can be felt particularly when he came to the core of his meditation, the point at which religious attention began to focus on God's descent to man: how God draws near to a human being.

Titus began his exposition with a reference to tradition. He wanted to speak to them "in the spirit of the fathers." With evident pride Titus then spoke of their own Dutch tradition – about the unique significance of it which had been of great influence on the spiritual life of the Netherlands and far beyond its borders.

In his statement of defense (January 1942), in which he explained why the Catholic church of the Netherlands rejected the

Dutch Nazi party, he had struck precisely the same note. This must have been music in the ears of the men who had been taken prisoner by virtue of their loyalty to the country. Titus Brandsma related how different religious types had developed over the years. He explained where the roots lay of the Dutch mystical tradition and how a remarkable shift occurred in people's religious outlook in the 16th century. He dealt at length with the religious type that arose in the 15th century and that was further developed in the Modern Devotion. From the time of Meister Eckhart believing people had sought God in his majesty. The whole focus was on God as the Holy One in whom there is an inexpressible fullness of life. In the following period religious attention shifted to the God who comes down, who searches for human beings. It was especially the distress of the times which prompted this shift in people's searching and thinking. It was distress which made itself felt on many levels: numerous disputes between the cities, the immense suffering brought on by the plague, and the disastrous consequences of the Western schism. It is from within their pain and distress that people raise the most fundamental questions. They cannot live with the suffering whose meaning escapes them. "Spirituality has its roots in our distress."[40] Here we are at the core of the meditation on Good Friday. How can you make sense in your life of suffering that is inescapable? How can you keep yourself from being crushed by it? How can you learn to bear it? The physician, Dr. H. Grond of Deventer, recorded on July 3, 1946, how, as Titus's fellow prisoner at the time, he had understood the core of this meditation. He relates how hundreds of people were packed together in a stuffy smoky room, barrack III A, a motley crowd consisting of professors and gypsies, believers and unbelievers, all dressed in the same slovenly jail outfits.

Standing before these people on Good Friday April 3, 1942, Titus Brandsma spoke about "Geert Grote and the idea of suffering." Small and fragile, he stood there in his faded uniform, propping

---

[40] H. Andriessen, Spiritualiteit als modern verhaal, Titus Brandsmalezing, Nijmegen 1994.

himself up between two bunks. In a weak monotonous tone of voice he spoke in a deathly quiet space where hundreds eagerly lapped up his words about divine mercy and love and the human willingness to make sacrifices. Without any rhetorical flourishes, and – I would say – camouflaging his great erudition, he spoke words of simple wisdom which found their way, from heart to heart, to his audience. He depicted for us medieval man, bewildered by the many deep and contradictory experiences he underwent. Natural disasters and grace, spiritual ecstasy and sin, witchcraft and the incomprehensible powers of nature were for medieval man experiences he had to undergo at a deep level, without any insight in the connection between them, with only a firm faith in God's mighty guidance. The task of Geert Grote and the Brothers of the Common Life, accordingly, lay not so much in the education of youth in a scholarly sense as in offering a firm guideline for people's life; and this firm guideline was the "daily consideration of Christ's suffering." And this Titus Brandsma held out to us as powerful support in our difficulties: daily meditation on God's suffering for us, by which our suffering for him can only mean joy. In his wounds we would find healing. It was a much-heard truth, therefore, but one which in these surroundings became for us a totally new source of inspiration, which enabled us to go forward with love where, humanly speaking, only hatred could exist. Because of these words alone, the last words which many of us would hear from him, Titus Brandsma's life, his priesthood, and his imprisonment were full of meaning.

Inner freedom

After the speech the prisoners went back to their barracks in silence. "I will never forget this man" (J. Donkers, 13-11-1945).

Remarkable, too, is what Colonel Fogtelo had seen. "It was as if this man was in the free world." By it he touched – insofar as it is possible to find words for it – the most profound fabric of our existence. Many who knew the appalling suffering of that time felt as if we humans were delivered up to unknown forces which do not obey our logic. This colonel saw that the man who spoke on suffering that Good Friday was not in the grip of unknown blind forces but lived in a freedom which came across as a gift.

When the colonel recognized this freedom in a world wracked by violence, he was discovering something new, a new kind of freedom. It is not possible to fathom the depth and the scope of it. We can only list a few of its characteristics.

Titus separated himself from his expectations, from his own constructs. This is how a person gets to live in the right relation to that which is most essential.

Freed from grim self-effort and fear, he was receptive to the power that comes from God. In that state his receptivity was great. There awakened in him a new power, one he recognized as coming from God, a power that enabled him to grow above and beyond himself. The most mysterious aspect of this is that he was now more himself than ever before. "He speaks as a person who lives in freedom." It is a new freedom, an enduring freedom which no one could take from him.

Soon after the message of Titus Brandsma the facts again asserted themselves. The hour in which a person prays and the hour in which he curses sometimes lie close together. The same week a group of Russians was executed. A day later virtually the whole camp population was forced to witness the pronouncement of the death sentences of more than 70 people from the resistance (the so-called O.D., the ministry of order, from Block IV). "From half past one to half past three they stood lined up in formation for this purpose in the parade ground. When that time had passed, the group from Block IV stepped up to the front, surrounded by a couple of hundred soldiers. For almost an hour they stood there facing each other in silence. This was the last act staged by the Nazis. They did not understand their mistake; this was much more impressive and of a different order than they expected. Among the prisoners there were some who folded their hands and pointed upward. Then a column of police vans drove in through the gate and onto the parade ground."[41] On May 3 the men of the first "O.D. trial" in Sachsenhausen, Oranienburg, were executed.

[41] H. W. Aukes, *Titus Brandsma*, Utrecht 1985, 264.

When Titus was about to receive a penal sentence, a few fellow prisoners, physicians, managed to obtain a medical certificate which secured for him a light job with the room watch. "There Titus could recover. He had time for it till Monday April 27. Then, through some mysterious channel, he learned that the authorities in The Hague were considering his transfer to Germany. That would be the end, Titus knew. That night he could not sleep. A teacher from Oude Tonge, Paul, who lay next to him in the bunk, felt sorry for him when, after a firm handshake and a word of encouragement, he heard his neighbor mumble one chaplet after another."[42]

Learning patience

At this time of testing things became too heavy for Titus. That is clear from a poem he wrote in Amersfoort.

> Grief would come and lay me low,
> No chance to make it go away,
> Nor with any tears allay,
> Else had I done it long ago.
> Then it came and on me weighed,
> Till I lay still and no more wept,
> Learned to watch and patience kept;
> Thereafter it no longer stayed.
> All that is passed and set aside;
> From far away I still recall
> And cannot understand at all
> That ancient grief nor why I cried.

This poem is interesting because it is one of the rare personal statements in which Titus Brandsma, in a few spare words, tells how heavy his suffering had become for him. A time arrived in which he felt trapped and was in a state of shock. All comfort had vanished. These are the only words familiar to us from Titus Brandsma in which he indicated that for a short time his suffering was too much for him.

---

[42] B. Meyer, o. carm., *Titus Brandsma*, Bussum 1951, 423.

There are splendid poems about which we cannot say anything except that they are splendid. And there are less splendid poems about which we can have interesting discussions.

So writes Herman de Coninck in "The Comfort of Pessimism."[43] Titus Brandsma's poem undoubtedly belongs to the latter category. It is a text without literary pretensions: it is about what it literally states.

Titus Brandsma's texts are, as a rule, devoid of heaviness. For him the life of everyday, however full of activities and cares, was never a hard burden. His speeches never reflected the mood of a tormented person. He did not like sowing unrest and doubt, as those do who continually raise all kinds of questions without wanting an answer. It was totally in keeping with his nature to discuss developments that are hopeful. The letters he wrote from prison were always gentle and full of a confidence that one day everything would come out right. The gentle tone of his letters kept the pain of shocking events hidden. The text of the poem printed above is an exception. We now know from himself how much he suffered. Although suffering is opposed to everything, it is nevertheless always and everywhere present – sometimes unbearably and inescapably so. The repeatedly returning "why" in Psalm 43 is both moving and terrifying.

> You, O God, were once my refuge –
> why have you cast me off?
> Why do I go about in mourning
> while my enemy has power?

There are many questions but the darkness continues. That is why the first thing that usually arises in us is protest. People complain and fend off suffering. Picasso's protest, depicted in the Guernica painting, is very poignant. It is a cry of dread over deadly violence. The wide-open mouth of the horse, the ugliness, the brutal signs of conflict – everything is a protest. The painting is all the more shocking for its portrayal of human powerlessness. Titus, however,

---

[43] H. de Coninck, *Over de troost van het pessimisme*, Antwerpen, 115.

found an attitude which goes beyond protest. It represents a power which breaks the spell and an acceptance which confers a deep independence and frees him from his unsteady self.

What comes across in this poem is not the language of power. It is the language of a person who has been sidelined, who is no longer a factor to be reckoned with, but who has nevertheless positioned himself in reality in a way that is entirely his own, which, consequently, is still there. He has his memories of past years, memories of a well-ordered life of praying and working, and the security he found there. Now he has found a new security which no one can take from him because they themselves do not know this security,.

Until his arrest Titus enjoyed a life filled with activities. He knew the deep meaning and salutary nature of a world in which people give shape, in a tried-and-tested culture of connectedness, to the essential values of life. People lived in a wholesome rhythm of reflection, labor, and prayer. As a result of the experience of God there was a solid center. Now he is forced to subject himself to arbitrariness without illusions, and is alone with all the energies which he can no longer focus on his many daily activities.

When a person assumes he no longer has any meaningful connections and is afraid of being alone, he will discover that his life is not meaningless the moment he realizes that there are people who need him. This realization does not depend on the success of his dealings with other people. When he takes someone's fate to heart, he also discovers that the fullness of life's meaning does not consist in what a person receives from life, but in what he has to give. In the process of acting on his concern the course of his life becomes clear. A person's desire, after all, is not always clear. Formation is needed. The fact that people claim him helps him focus his desire. Seeing that other people need him enables Titus all the better to cope with the absolutely meaningless character of the brutal life in a death camp.

As Titus later admitted in a letter, that first period in Scheveningen had not been easy. When in Scheveningen he wrote that he felt happy, we know that he also acutely felt the negative side of being a prisoner. Life behind barred doors; the humiliation and violence of this life; wanting to jump up in fury over the injustice of it all; being powerless to change even one iota of the situation: that is the core of suffering.

Physical pain as a rule leaves no scars on the soul of a person. Titus knew what it meant to be forced to live with chronic physical pain. He seldom even mentioned the hardships involved in it. His passion for work was never affected by it. Now, however, he was confronted in a heavy-handed way with a very different kind of suffering: injustice, contempt, hatred. "Then it came and weighed me down." This is the image of a great weight of suffering, the weight of a tombstone. Suffering threatened to crush him. He lay still, without weeping, entirely in the grip of suffering: mute, strange, empty. It was only for a brief time, but a brief time can last forever, an unreal moment between time and eternity.

If he had told us in that first period that he felt offended, trampled on, in that tiny jail cell, we would not have been surprised. Misfortune is experienced in all its brutal weight at the moment it strikes and can only be processed and accepted over time. Titus experienced that his suffering was irresistible. It was impossible to fend it off or "allay it with tears." There was no way to escape the torment of hunger and cold, the anxieties attending exposure. At the same time he also experienced a kind of security. In his inmost self he found comfort. People might hurt his exterior life; they could not touch his innermost. When his final support from without had been withdrawn, when he had nothing left to cling to and was divested of all protection, he again discovered a security that the outside world could not disturb, or take from him, or even touch.

It is not the naïve certainty of one who refused to see the danger. It is rather the security which arises from the certainty that he is being heard by Someone who is near. When he prayed and stammered out words of distress and pain from a vital sense of God's nearness, these words were not lost in a sea of nothingness. He knew they were being heard. This security is imbedded in the all-embracing presence of God.

Then it came and on me weighed,
Till I lay still and no more wept,
Learned to watch and patience kept;
Thereafter it no longer stayed.

"Waiting and being patient," he learned to accept this inescapable suffering by trusting in God's hidden powers. With his thoughts he focused on God, stammering and praying. His words, as we said a moment ago, are not solitary vocables perishing in the nothingness of a passing means of support. His patience and waiting are indicative of his willingness to accept suffering. Meaninglessness cannot be the last word. Waiting patiently, he will find the answer to the suffering that has struck him – an answer he will give with his whole self. He is saying here that something is happening to him which is beyond him but at the same time occurs as a human possibility in his life. He was aware that it could not be exacted by tears; he had to wait. Yet it did not occur apart from him and he experienced it as something that was profoundly characteristic of him.

Italo Calvino, speaking of the powers from without which set in motion things that are deeply ingrained in a person's mind, employs the image of a riverbed. He calls it the sand bed which forms a deposit on the river bottom of his thoughts. "Every grain of the sand of the spirit preserves a moment of life and deposits it in such a way that it can no longer be erased but is buried under innumerable other grains."[44] Sometimes there is a protrusion in the riverbed which produces "whirlpools" in the stream which may set in motion the powers slumbering there. The powers to accept suffering, not to let oneself be robbed of good cheer and the capacity to see clearly, may be released in the tumultuous days of grief and dread.

To wait and be patient does not, however, mean that it occurs all by itself without any activity on his part. Needed are inner concentration and a continual drive to be released from the instinct of self-preservation. It will happen to him as an incalculable favor.

---

[44] I. Calvino, De weg naar San Giovanni, Amsterdam 1992, 53.

A person who has thus experienced this acceptance as a favor and himself as altogether open and desirous of this favor can say of himself that he is happy in his cell. To be patient means: not to let the wounds which result from the realization of the good rob him of good cheer and the capacity to see clearly. Precisely by the express acceptance of grief and confusion of heart patience protects a person from having his spirit broken by grief and losing its greatness. Patience sustains a radiant inwardness in a state of profound "unhurtness." Patience, as Hildegard of Bingen puts it, is "the pillar which is mollified by nothing." And Thomas, mirroring Holy Scripture (Luke 21:19), sums up with splendid aptness the virtue of patience: "By patience a human being possesses his soul."[45] It seems contradictory that this man, who had been involved in so many different activities, should arrive at acceptance by – above all – an attitude of expectancy. This attitude embraces an openness and receptivity which is without vagueness.

It is an openness with a passion for and sensitivity to the secret of life. It is a secret that in the final analysis we do not belong to ourselves: there both our origin and destiny is *given* to us. In his acceptance discourse as rector of the Catholic University of Nijmegen on the "image of God" Titus says that we must look for the secret of our origin "first of all in ourselves. God is there and reveals himself to us there. He wants to be seen and recognized there. He is, after all, nowhere more clearly knowable to us than in the ground of our being."[46] Here something happens that cannot be demanded by force. Since he is open to the secret of life, forces are awakened in him which bear the character of graciousness. Patience and watchfulness keep Titus from slipping into a comfortless abyss. Nothing is worse than disconsolateness because it implies the abandonment of life. When he has been deprived of everything, he arrives at the ultimate experience – the core of his life – that, empty of everything, he is now being filled with the comfort of God's nearness, a comfort which is incalculably deep

---

[45] J. Pieper, De zin van de dapperheid, Hilversum 1960, 33.
[46] B. Borchert, Mystiek leven, Een bloemlezing, Nijmegen 1985, 106, 108.

and to which he had no access in any other way. "I can cry out with jubilant joy," Titus wrote in one of his letters.

Patience does not mean the exclusion of an energetic approach. Openness also has the character of availability, keeping oneself open to completely different claims of life. Titus, after all, had completely relinquished his own will and plans and now strongly experienced the space made free by that relinquishment: he is now inwardly available to that which comes out to meet him from without. Titus freed himself from himself: all his attention now goes out to the suffering of the other. Not being available, says Gabriel Marcel, is to be preoccupied with oneself.

> All that is passed and set aside;
> From far away I still recall
> And cannot understand at all
> That ancient grief nor why I cried.

In the first stanza we saw a Titus that is very different from the one we know from his writings. In the third stanza he found himself back again. His tears have dried and he is amazed. It is as if he was a different man then. His heart has been freed from an oppressive burden. He underwent this process without resistance. His amazement sounds matter-of-fact. In this way, apparently, he wanted to keep his emotions somewhat at a distance.

He recovered his firmness and with it the power to bear everything that was about to follow as a result of it. Often such a process is realized in hardness and impassiveness, and many soon get caught up in a situation of reciprocal hard-heartedness. This recovery of one's true basis, however, can also crystallize spiritually into an attitude which radiates great inner peace. It can only occur in a setting of the profoundest piety. Titus, after all, could only arrive at this inner acceptance if for him there was an ultimate reality hidden behind this tangible world, one which is more stable and timeless and to which a person can give his ultimate trust. It is an acceptance full of hope. Titus suffered with tears, but he recovered his strength, his independence, and the radiant core of his personality. His smile came back, a profound expression of his humanity, just as his tears had been a poignant expression of humanity. On Wednesday morning April 28, at the crack of dawn around 6 a.m., the prison van came by to take Herr Professor Titus Brandsma to the third room of the press division on the Binnenhof where "S.S. Hauptscharführer" Hardegen would again cross-examine him.

10. Condemned to Death

In Hardegen's second interrogation the subject matter concerned Titus Brandsma's most important activities: the Catholic university, Catholic secondary education, the Catholic daily press, his opposition to discrimination against the Jews. For Titus Brandsma the interests he had sincerely promoted were so unquestionably sound and holy that he did not feel any need to rethink his position. Survivors of the camps later remembered that Titus repeatedly indicated that, were he again to become embroiled in such a situation, he would act the same way.

After this interrogation, when late in the evening Titus arrived at "Hotel Orange" in Scheveningen, the cell door again opened for him with much grating of keys. The cell, however, was already occupied. Two young men looked at him with intense curiosity. The cell, after all, was small and cramped. An additional occupant could be a problem. Titus, the men found, looked very frail. They designated the only bed in the cell for him. They themselves could manage with an old mattress on the floor. These men were De Graaf and Oostdijck. C. De Graaf later wrote a "memorandum: memories of sharing a cell with Professor Titus Brandsma."

> Late in the evening one day in April 1942 our cell door (no. 623) was flung open and with cries of "los, los" ("Get going! Get going!") a third cell mate was, as it were, thrown in among us. Since it was already dark we could not so easily make out who it was. Soon, however, we introduced ourselves. We found we had with us one of the greatest men of the Catholic faith, a man who had fallen into the hands of the "Huns" precisely because of his faith and trust in God. After talking a bit more, we fixed a bed for the prof, who was very tired, exceedingly thin, and obviously weak. The prof came Wednesday from Amersfoort where he had lain in bed with dysentery for six weeks – hence his bad condition. In the morning we had an

opportunity to get further acquainted. We were amazed at all the things the prof had smuggled inside with him: a pocket knife, a fountain pen, a pair of scissors, pencils, a mirror and more such little items which, despite everything, can still make life in a cell somewhat more pleasant. We ourselves possessed a watch and something to smoke, so our equipment was pretty good. The prof began to tell us some stories and with that a large part of the day passed by. For me, who had already been a prisoner since October 41, it was a great relief to have the prof with us. I'm just an ordinary guy, as they call it, and so when you get to meet a scholar like prof. Brandsma, that cheers you up and contributes to your general education. The prof told us a good deal about trips he had made, also about his visit to Theresia Neumann who at certain times experienced the suffering of Christ. He also told us about the origin and history of the Carmelites, Benedictines, Franciscans, and other orders. Also about the life of Teresa of Avila, Francis of Assisi, Geert Grote and many more of these great figures. In the evening after we ate, we always played cards for about an hour; then the prof prayed again and so it gradually became time to forget our cares in sleep. Sunday morning we had a meditation and prayer. Also on Ascension Day prof held a service – those were really great moments in our life. Sometimes, with the help of the floor guard and the assistant floor guard, the prof got an extra cup of milk and in the afternoon an extra pot of something. Especially the assistant floor guard did his best. The prof knew his father well and him too somewhat. It was a certain Nieuwenhuyzen from Amersfoort. One day the prof was picked up at 9 a.m. for an interrogation on the Binnenhof and not brought back till 7 p.m. He spent several hours in the cellar of course, and had had no food, but we kept food warm for him so that he could still go to bed with a full stomach. The prof was given paper, a pen, and ink and then had to write down why he was against the Germans. I can't remember anymore what the document said, but it came down to the point that he did not oppose them because they were Germans but because of the Nazi regime, the oppressors of faith and spiritual freedom, who poisoned the people and especially youth with their propaganda. The prof wrote this piece in duplicate, one copy going to the Binnenhof and one he kept for himself.

For me the prof wrote a poem: "To Jesus," with his own pen, and undersigned it with his signature. On Friday afternoon the prof was told that he was going to be transferred on Saturday; that was postponed for a week, but on Saturday the trip took place anyway and so the prof left never to see Holland again. Still we may not mourn over this. He himself knew it would not last much longer and he longed for the salvation he now enjoys before the throne of his Redeemer.

In those 18 days which they spent together, locked up in a cell that was far too small, a brief and delicate friendship arose which for a time lifted them above the hopelessness of their fate. Together they looked at the world around them and reflected on God's hidden presence in it. Such a friendship is stronger than time.

On May 6 the interrogations ended. The relentless verdict read: "Deportation to Dachau, Germany, for the entire duration of the war! There is a telephone. If you want to you can cell Nijmegen to give them this information." When the connection had been made, Titus's message was:

> Yes, pater prior, really with pater Titus, you must know! At this moment I am at the office of the ministry of security in The Hague. I was cross-examined again. The authorities have decided to send me to Dachau, one of the largest concentration camps in Germany. This does mean that I will probably be kept there till the end of the war.... No – do not worry about me. At the moment I am doing very well and I will have no trouble making it, I believe. Many greetings to all my friends and acquaintances. More I cannot say at this time. Bye, Bye!

Early in the morning on Saturday May 16, a number of prisoners from the police prison in Scheveningen stood ready for the trip to Kleve, a transit station on the way to Dachau. The specter of the death camp was coming closer. The bonds which had grown so rapidly and were a source of ultimate security for the prisoners in their isolation were broken with equal rapidity.

In the grip of fear

In the course of that Saturday, May 16, Titus Brandsma arrived in Kleve and was dropped off in the convict prison, a somewhat

somber-looking building located on the edge of this German bor-
der town. Nazi formalism had not yet completely taken over in
this prison. The director, Baron Von Ketteler, proved to be a decent
man. The guards were still from before the time of the Nazis. The
prisoners were entrusted by the secret police to the prison's own
personnel. The Gestapo did not even have keys to the building but
had "permission" now or later to speak with prisoners or to take
them along with them. There was one man, a police constable,
who now and then dealt roughly with the prisoners. When he
noticed that Titus had made a cross of strips of paper and had
pasted it to the inside of the cell door, he offered his commentary
in coarse terms. Titus, though not deeply impressed by it, took a
somewhat more cautious approach and used white paper and
pasted it against the wall bearing the words: *stat crux:* "though all
things waver, the cross remains our hope."

In this prison, though the atmosphere was somewhat more
favorable, the days became very heavy for Titus. The specter of
exhaustion and a lonely death drew threateningly closer. He was
now crossing a dark threshold: Was return still possible? The injustice of his situation was all the more striking. He lost his deep
inner peace. Fear attacked him, fear that rendered him powerless.
The protective power of a well-ordered inner life no longer func-
tioned. The spring within no longer produced living water. Fear
had him by the throat. He could no longer be reached. Titus sank
away in an experience that up until then had been totally foreign
to him. Darkness set in as it did in the night of the Garden of
Olives. A sense of irreversible doom came over him. His fate, empty
and devoid of meaning, no longer had anything human about it.
He had no connection with it: it was hard and without mercy.

The gray wall of the cell only meant that he was a prisoner.
Though there were others in his cell, Titus felt lonelier than ever.
He shared his cell with an Italian NCO, with a citizen of Utrecht
named R.J. de Groot, with a greengrocer who now worked in
the prison kitchen, and with the Rev. Johan Kapteyn from
Groningen. In a conversation with De Groot Titus said: "I'm sure
you will be freed. But I – I will share the fate of pastor Galama and

chaplain Van Rooijen of 's-Heerenberg. They were transferred to Dachau and died there." His fellow prisoners no longer saw him smile. People often noticed that his thin cheeks were stained with tears.

The days in Kleve were not like those in Scheveningen. There Titus experienced his days as he did in his monastic cell on the Doddendaal in Nijmegen. Then the cell was a symbol of "being at home," an image of inwardness and purity from which he recognized and accepted the world around him. His most inward thoughts could always return there to a moment of intimacy with God.

In the prison at Kleve this sacred, all-embracing moment was lacking. There Titus noted that his spiritual life was declining, an observation that deeply shocked him. It meant the loss of the best and most certain element within him. In Kleve he lost the serenity and comfort of which he was full when, while in Scheveningen, he wrote: "O Jesus, when I look on you."

Inwardness had always given great stability to his life, whatever the circumstances in which he found himself. But now, so far from being a source of ongoing blessing, it became a specter and brought him into a twilight of uncertainty. It made him fearful and sad. Fear isolates and monopolizes a person. For a time Titus was "beside himself" and no longer knew what to do with his dread. He entered into a battle with himself and tried to fend off a violent death in a concentration camp. He was restless: Was there still hope? Was it possible to escape deportation to Dachau? Or was all hope vain at this point? His friends were all far away; God who was always so near, kept silent. He wanted to leave this evil existence. Being alone was utter abandonment now. He anxiously held onto a last little glimmer of hope. There had to be a way out.

It was not in Titus's nature to expand on his fear and grief and to look for sympathy. He did, however, feel the need for an intimate personal conversation. The man who had learned from experience what detachment and relinquishment meant was now concerned over his own fate. Earlier, when there were obstinate problems at the university, people had always called on Brandsma to fix them. Now the darkness was so intense he could no longer do much with his clear and peaceful mind. The oppressiveness of the oppressor was too much for him. Everything within him began to rise up in rebellion. Now he was the weaker party seeking help. In this final stopping point before landing in Dachau he could not overcome his fear.

It is clear that he did not endure his suffering like a stoic. It was not like him to confront evil with a rock-hard and superior attitude. He wanted to share himself with a person who would listen to him, understand him, and empathize with him.

In those days – days without light and comfort – Titus talked much with the prison chaplain Ludwig Deimel. Chaplain Deimel was a vicar at one of Kleve's parishes. Every other day Deimel visited him and under the guise of confession could take him to the sacristy and have long talks with him about his study. He loaned out books to Titus, among others, Romano Guardini's *Das Harren der Schöpfung*, a title which can be translated as "looking forward with trust and perseverance to the completion of creation." Referring to the promise that resounds from the entire Apocalypse, Guardini writes: "Over and over those who are afflicted and in conflict are told: 'Persevere! Remain faithful! And an immeasurable fulfillment will be your portion.'" In those conversations with Deimel and reading that book, did Titus see that there are depths of even greater darkness than his own?

He felt totally unprotected, abandoned to a violent plan. Darkness settled in his soul. The shutters had been slammed shut. The cell which once has been intensely meaningful to him had lost its meaning. The austere walls surrounding him now sealed him off. Not one familiar thing any longer got to him. There was no longer a cell in which he could be alone and find rest.

Is there still a way out?

Deeply tired, he rose from his seat. In this over-populated cell he had to look for a quiet spot to write some notes in preparation for a petition for a reduction of his sentence. On narrow strips of paper he wrote about his condition with a firm hand. He wrote that he was beginning to lose his memory. He could no longer even pray the Our Father. He could no longer recall the two Psalms he prayed every day. He no longer knew the name of the philosopher who most inspired him. Later that name came back to him so that he could insert it: Henri Bergson. "But how do I save these slips of paper," he wondered. There was no privacy here of any kind. Then the solution came to him: in the lining of his hat. No one would look for them there. What he had written would remain hidden there till after the war.

When, after his death, the Nazis sent his suitcase with his clothes back to the monastery in Nijmegen, his hat was included. The prior of the monastery was delighted to see it. At the time there was a dearth of everything. With that hat he could take one step forward again. However, it did not fit him. The prior knew a competent hat maker. When, however, the latter heard that the hat had belonged to Titus Brandsma he felt a strong and reverent desire for that hat. He venerated Titus as a saint. He would let the prior pick out a brand new Borselino if only he could keep Titus's hat. Mr. Boers, the hat maker, got the hat and the prior happily returned to his monastery. Soon the rumor went around that Titus's hat was being kept as a relic in the home of the Boers family. There are always enough people who feel that in such a venerable relic there may possibly be healing powers. An old lady in the neighborhood heard the rumor. She was tormented by rheumatic pains which made her fingers crooked and rigid. Full of hope she rang the doorbell. If she were allowed to touch this hat with deeper inner devotion something might happen which no doctor was capable of. And indeed, she thought she discerned a feeling of well-being in her fingers when she handled the hat intimately and firmly. She did not, however, handle the hat very gently with the result that something broke. Strips of paper came twirling out, the little strips which Titus had hidden behind the sweatband and behind the black ribbon....

The slips contain his hidden cries of fear. They are the only texts in which Titus speaks of his own spiritual suffering. He wrote them as a preliminary draft of his petition for a reduction of his sentence. The petition is dated June 12, 1942, the day before his transfer to Dachau.

Titus's revulsion from being delivered up to the appalling world of the Nazis grew stronger. Accordingly, he conceived a plan that would seem plausible to the German authorities who had the power to decide his fate. He knew very well that there was little room or compassion in the views of the Nazis. In consultation with the prison chaplain, and in drawing up a petition for a reduction of his sentence, his frail health seemed to him a sound argument. He suffered from an intestinal disorder and after his arrest had to go without his prescribed medicines. In his petition Titus drew up an impressive list of physical and mental ailments to persuade the Germans that "… it seems hardly possible in a prison or a camp to make the exceptions which the undersigned needs if his health is not to continue to be seriously threatened."

In a letter addressed to the monastery in Doddendaal Titus wrote: "The provincial could try to get it changed through a transfer to a German monastery (Mainz, Vienna, Bamberg, Straubing), if necessary with a severe curtailment of my freedom…. Some time ago Father Bulters from The Hague was also released on condition of a transfer to Venray. It seems to me best to discuss this in The Hague (main office of the German Security Service, Binnenhof 7) with Hardegen, Room 127. The latter regularly cross-examined me. He told me that Mr. Brandsma of Zwolle had also been there on my behalf and that he had given him my large traveling case. For the rest, it seems to me he did not succeed in getting many concessions either, but I am nevertheless very grateful for his efforts. This time too he could go there to discuss the issue, either alone or with the Provincial or his deputy. This last suggestion does not seem bad to me but I am happy to leave the matter to you." It took three weeks before this letter, mailed on May 28, reached its destination. A few days earlier, Deimel had found a certain Hezewijk, an iron merchant who regularly came to the Netherlands for business, willing to seek contact with the prior of the Carmelites in Nijmegen. We know that the prior of his monastery, along with Mr. Brandsma, traveled to The Hague. However, all attempts at saving Titus from Dachau continued to be fruitless.

When Titus understood that his attempt to get his sentence changed was futile, he felt the clammy hand of fate on his neck. He simply had to go through a dark night of solitude and helplessness. He first had to experience this darkness before he could say in deep confidence: "...not mine but your will be done." Now that his suffering affected him so deeply a glimmer of new insight dawned on him. His salvation and freedom were of a totally different nature. They were bound up with the shocking realization that he must relinquish all expectation that someone would put his hand on his shoulder and save him from this appalling world.

Titus's days in the prison cell in Kleve were among the darkest of his life. It was a phase in his life through which many pass and experience as sheer horror. In Scheveningen Titus felt something of this heaviness when, locked in his cell, he chose the text "pati and contemni," "to suffer and be despised." These words came from John of the Cross, a sixteenth-century Carmelite who wrote very movingly about the dark night of the soul. "I had no other light than that which burned in my heart. This guided me more surely than the light of noon".[47]

Those who seek God with a certain passion and solely focus their life on him will encounter a cross on their way and experience that suffering does not destroy life but preserves and purifies it, so that it can again rise afresh. Those who seek God will inevitably experience a time of darkness and purifying pain. This dark night is not just there when life is against us and makes us despondent. The dark night of the soul is much more. Those who seek God initially assume they know the way they must go. They know where they must seek God. They are on the right road and feel happy. All of a sudden, however, there comes a time, totally unexpectedly, when everything turns out differently. They became disturbed at being confronted by the unfathomable

[47] Stanzas 3-4 of *The Ascent of Mount Carmel.*

mystery of life. Alarm dims their view of reality. The space of perception becomes ever smaller; nothing remains other than an inner
perception of a sign. There is no other comfort than this inner
capacity for listening; it is precisely suffering which gradually
refines this capacity. In this inmost interiority the most hidden
secrets between God and man are revealed. Saint John of the Cross
experienced this in a special way. About it he wrote: "O guiding
night! O night more lovely than the dawn" [48].

The inapprehensible dimension concealed behind everything is
to one person a fate completely empty and without purpose.
To many others it is a mystery, a higher power, a divine ordinance.
Titus tasted this powerlessness in silence. In the silence of his last
days in Kleve hope of being rescued revived in him for a moment,
a final despairing cry for deliverance. He let go of this impotent
desire to save what could be saved. For one last time he longed for
the silence of the monastic cell where the hidden depths of life are
experienced. No answer came. His last hope evaporated. Titus was
*dis*illusioned. He was now a man who had nothing left to expect.
In this Mount of Olives, where he was deprived of everything,
it dawned on him that he was being asked to relinquish his own
expectations. Reality revealed to him its hard, unyielding side.
He could not possibly escape that reality. All resistance was point-
less and could only inflame his sense of powerlessness and lead him
deeper into despair.

There is another road – a road many people lack the courage to
take. That road opens up when people leave events to themselves,
take incalculability for what it is – as something that can neither
be avoided nor managed. Titus reached that point of relinquishment, and that meant to relinquish himself. Those who do this
out of love recover themselves in a new way. Those who relinquish
themselves to God find themselves again as they have never been
before, but do recognize themselves. They find the most essential
nature of their existence that lies deeply concealed in the unknown
depths of their life.

---

[48] Stanza 5.

Titus's suffering did not destroy his life but preserved and purged it, so that it could arise again as something new.

Titus's self-knowledge increased. He had experienced himself as a person who had lost all his connections and been overcome by fear – fear of spiritual decline, powerlessness, a horrible death. Based on his view of faith he knew that external prestige is not the true way that leads to a valid image of man. The mind of faith teaches how one must view man. Experience teaches who he really is. Titus discovered how he himself had to consent to this loss and that he was a small and vulnerable human being, that this was the truth of his life, that he had to acknowledge this or else fall a prey to fear. He was now the person about whom in the thirties he had spoken with so much reverence: a man in his humiliation. "God chose what is weak in the world to shame the strong": the threatened insecure person who is always more than he can credit himself with being but is also quick to escape the truth of his life.

Titus knew how decisively important it is not to look back once a person has put his hand to the plow (Luke 9:62); those who live their lives always looking back over their shoulder will make a mess of their life. For him the past in which he was of great importance for many was not now an instrument of self-preservation. He ventured to take the days ahead as they came. In so doing he completed, in an unprecedented way, what he had imposed on himself in Scheveningen. A little strip of paper on the wall of his prison cell was meant to remind him of it: "Take the days as they come." The phrase "as they come," however, meant that he especially wanted to involve himself more deeply and passionately with those days. He accepted the days of his imprisonment in the expectation that in that period of darkness he would probably be even more receptive to the mystery of God's nearness. Thus Titus regained a firm footing in the shocking and utterly unforeseen movement of his life. In a new and purified way, this gave him rest.

It is impossible to describe, in all-embracing language, what was happening in the most intimate hiddenness of Titus's inner life when in his case the final resistance broke down and he surrendered and rose to a new life. When a person inwardly agrees to relinquish control over his fate, it seems to him that he faces a vacuum. That word suggests something spatial. It is an image. It means that in the process of relinquishment one increasingly loses his bearings and finally no longer has any ground beneath his feet and threatens to fall into a bottomless space. For Titus it meant surrendering everything to him who is greater than we and will not drop us. To surrender everything to a purpose which transcends one's own: acceptance.

Acceptance deprives events of their fatal character. Longing, disillusionment, and acceptance are not three stages through which a person passes sequentially. We are not talking here of a temporal order. All three are simultaneously present. If he can accept that there will no longer be a homecoming, no "cella continuata," the desire for it will nevertheless remain and the disillusionment over the nonrealization of a final consolation will continue to torment him. By the acceptance of life in its limited character and in its incalculability death has to occur already in this life.

To be at home nowhere. At the end of his life Titus relinquished the desire to be at home in his cell. In this respect he was walking in the footsteps of the first Carmelites who lived in the awesome silence and grandeur of Mount Carmel and, having been driven from that location by the Saracens, went to Europe in order, wherever that might be, to experience the silence and grandeur of Carmel. They were never to find a fixed dwelling place again and, guided solely by the desire of their heart, went in search of the experience of God's nearness as they had known it on Mount Carmel.

The final journey

Titus Brandsma went from one halfway house to another, never settled in one place, had no cell which offered him protection and where he could be happy. He did this with no other comfort than God's nearness. On June 16, 1942, Titus, along with the Rev. Johan Kapteyn, was dispatched to Dachau.

They took their last journey to the death camp of Dachau without dreams and without a future. Titus walked with Pastor Kapteyn, his left wrist shackled to the right wrist of this congenial gentleman with whom he shared a cell in Kleve. There was both astonishment and fear in their eyes. They looked at the streets, the houses, and the shops where life followed its daily course. They were struck deep in their soul.

At the station in Kleve the train to Frankfurt stood ready for departure. At the end of the long train, behind the baggage car, a special railway car had been attached. The people on the station platform who were watching recognized it as the "Zellenwagen" (the cell car). In it a number of cells had been constructed. Each cell occupied approximately one square meter, had a bench, and a swing-back little shelf which a person could call an improvised table. The window was tiny, of frosted glass, and heavily barred. It was, moreover, constructed quite high against the ceiling so that no one could look outside. One of the cells was designated for Titus Brandsma and Pastor Kapteyn.

Prisoners, thin as rails, were loaded onto the "Zellenwagen." Men in green uniforms looked on. It seemed these men did not know what was happening. They acted and looked as if this was normal.

It became a long journey from Kleve where they came from, packed as they were in a tiny "compartment" where all conveniences were lacking. Subsequently, along the way, the Belgian Jesuit pater Leon de Coninck and a priest from Eupen-Malmedy, Nicolas Lamboray, were also shoehorned into the same space so that now four persons were locked in a cell with actually had room only for two. The journey continued to Frankfurt-am-Main where they were "unloaded" to spend the night there. Here they encountered a fifth companion in adversity, a German clergyman named Heinrich Rupieper. And so they continued the trip now with five men jammed together. It was not long before it became sweltering hot in the tiny cell. The air was suffocating; the thirst unbearable. They knocked on the wall and kicked against the door to draw attention to their plight. Finally they heard someone stumbling closer. The door was cautiously opened about four or five inches. A guard looked searchingly inside, staring for a long time at each occupant. It seems he was amazed, but still hesitated. There are rules, after all… He disappeared. After some time, however, he returned with a pail of water. The door opened a crack, the chain remained. However inconveniently, they could drink. The water streamed down their chin over their filthy clothing.

In Nürnberg the train stopped. All were brought to "die Turn-halle" (gymnasium) where they had to stay three days. Then began the last leg of the journey which ended in Dachau. To the accom-paniment of the loud yells and curses of the SS men they were pushed along with others into the truck which stood ready. Jerk-ily the truck sped over the bumpy cobblestones through the town where, a few kilometers away from the center, the concentration camp was located.

Death Camp Dachau

Dachau is located 18 kilometers northeast of Munich in the Bavarian uplands. The camp, which goes back to 1938, is situated approximately a half hour's walk from the center of the town in the "Dachauer Moos," a swampy landscape, and surrounded by a huge complex of SS barracks and SS buildings. The prison camp is 600 meters long and 300 meters wide; on both sides of the camp alley are 17 barracks, each of which is 90 meters long.

The first inmates were communists. These prisoners had to build their prison themselves, surround themselves with electrically-charged barbed wire, a 2½ meter wide ditch, behind that again a 2½ to 3 meter high wall similarly covered by electrically-charged barbed wire, and watchtowers every 50 meters, from which they were subsequently threatened and shot at with machine guns. The concentration camp could by no means, not even from a great distance, be seen or observed by civilians. One first had to pass through the large SS camp which was blocked at intervals by gates and barriers before coming to a final barrier of highly electrically-charged barbed wire. Escape was out of the question. Anyone even

attempting escape over this wire became a charred corpse the moment he touched it.

The entrance consisted of a large archway made of stone with built-in rooms for offices, sentries and supervisors. In the archway was a heavy iron gate bearing in elegant letters the inscription: "Arbeit macht frei" ("Labor liberates"). The truth was that, though the prisoner might work ever so hard, he would not get his freedom back. To the east of this entrance was the large parade ground where every morning and evening thousands of dead-tired hungry-looking men stood lined up in perfectly straight rows of ten, next to and behind each other, waiting for the sign that the roll call was over.

Hanging heavily over the camp was an atmosphere of resignation and powerless submissiveness in which life sank to an unfathomably low level. The prisoners had been weakened by hunger and forced labor. The sheds for people were cold and clammy; surrounding them was mud and barbed wire. The prisoners looked in vain for a sign of recognition and felt extremely unsafe. As persons with the most tenuous grip on life they awaited the day of liberation. The only thing that kept them more or less afoot was the thought of getting through just that one day. The numerous tortures – such as standing still for hours on end, endlessly walking in circles, and the beatings when something went wrong – were all designed to break their will. Every day had a fixed rhythm: "ausrücken" ("going to work") and "einrücken" ("coming back"), in the prescribed order. Going to work in long lines; standing before a small pan of soup in long lines. It all had the appearance of an orderly existence. In fact the camp was a marginal area without any consolation, where human beings were deprived of everything and even their dreams were shattered.

Here Titus Brandsma entered another world where all his values were reversed. In his own world, as he viewed it in "the enclosed garden," the walls served as protection against threats from without. The walls protected people, so as not to be overpowered by violence and dread and could really live. Here the walls kept normal life at bay so that the inconceivable would remain invisible to the outside world.

When Titus arrived in Dachau he had been underway for six long days and nights. On Friday, June 19, he was brought into the camp through the large entryway. First he was housed in the Admission Block, later in barrack 28. He was given a red triangle to wear on his gray smock and above the triangle the number 30492. The professor was now a bare-shaven naked man. A number had been burnt into his arm. From this point on he had no name. He had been stripped of all dignity. Here Titus underwent the merciless brutality of camp life. Yet he conducted himself as if he lived in freedom. His inner silence, his final possession, was something no one could take from him. His few final words were a benediction and reminded degraded humans of life that is life indeed.

The hand of a friend

In the camp Titus had a special encounter. It was a fellow brother who was to surround him with much care. It was Raphael Tijhuis born in Rijssen (The Netherlands) in 1913. He lived in the Carmelite monastery in Mainz where he was taken prisoner at the beginning of the war. He was a tailor, concerned to see people make a good impression: they had to look good. He was sensitive on that issue. Raphael, a strong and robust man, survived all the fear and terrors of this period. After the war he wrote about it in his own modest way.

> On a given day I met chaplain Rothkrans who told me he had seen Titus Brandsma in the Admission Block. That was surprising news to me. Since in that early period he, like every other newcomer, had to spend some time in the Admission Block, we could not immediately get to speak with him. On our part, however, we left no stone unturned to get into touch with him; but the doorkeeper of the Admission Block acquitted himself well of the task of admitting no one from the camp through the gate; and so some time passed before we could persuade the man to let us welcome pater Titus. How old and thin he had become! His stay in the different prisons and camps had left their terrible marks on him. When I met him for the first

time he gave me a rather strange look, but soon he recognized, in the "criminal" dressed in zebra-striped clothing who stood in front of him, one of his own fellow brothers.[49]

In the Admission Block Titus had to learn to sing the most loathsome soldier ditties; he had to learn to march, and what the service ranks of the SS men were. Those days weighed like lead on him. What could he do there with his beloved motto: "Take the days as they come"? He sensed the boundary of human existence. Even hares have nests but for him there was no safe place and no protection. When Titus was taken to Block 28 it felt to his mind as if he was being liberated.

> Thank God I am now away from that hell. They just beat you, and kick you to the accompaniment of all those curses. I found that cursing just horrible. That was no life; at least now I am with you!" He said all this with obvious relief; yet we had to laugh and tried to make clear to him that for him the real Dachau life was only just beginning now. "However it may be, I'll do my best not to cause too much trouble for the gentlemen and be as inconspicuous as possible," he said.

Wherever this was in any way possible Titus and Raphael were to be together. They had much to give to each other: Titus's unflappable inner composure and Raphael's robust physical strength. Each of them in his own way resisted the cruelty and terror of those days. In this friendship there were several contrasts which, as this so often happens, were in conflict or in harmony with each other. The contrast became fruitful; their spiritual strengths became more intimate. The fact that the one was a professor and the other a tailor no longer mattered. In a death camp like Dachau people learn to adopt another order of looking and thinking. Externals, so important to the Nazis, lost their weight. They now encountered each other as persons, the unique nature and mystery of human persons. It was precisely the respect for each other as persons which bound them more closely together and which simultaneously created distance and furnished free space.

---

[49] Manuscript, Nederlands Carmelitaans Instituut Boxmeer.

In the report which Raphael wrote after the war the reader senses this respect as a pure counterforce to the merciless nature of the Nazi terror. In their encounters, for just a few precious moments, they felt protected against the cold wind of this terror. The consolation of brotherhood can make suffering more bearable and human. It cannot, however, take away the suffering. Those who suffer, suffer alone.

Each of the two in his own way saw the tragedy of life. They were astonished to see that human beings, in their powerful desire for friendship and love, for happiness and the highest attainable ideals, now turn this desire into a paradise, then again into a hell. Titus, being a born optimist, recorded his involvement in this in the drawing of "The Enclosed Garden," the image of a well put-together world. What fascinated him was the ideal image. Raphael, for his part, made a drawing of Dachau after the war. He was a realist and a keen observer. Something of the hideous image of the death camp remained behind in him. His drawing warns: "do not ever forget this!"

Now that Titus found himself caught up in the terror of Dachau, the acceptance of suffering meant for him a willingness to be destroyed by it. He always took the days as they came. This reinforced his own inner sense of order. He did not fall into despair, now that the days were singularly bad.

Unspeakable cruelties took place in the camp on a daily basis. A rationally thinking person did not know what to do with them. The suffering in the camp was merciless and absurd. Hunger, cold, beatings, leaden weariness, always the fear of death and the piles of emaciated naked bodies. In the literature of the death camps hunger is always mentioned as the greatest enemy of human resistance. We must realize that the reference is to hunger that cannot be driven out with a bowl of soup or a piece of bread. "This hunger is the greatest enemy of human resistance."[50] Hunger eats away at the human sense of being responsible for each other. Hunger transforms people into brutal egoists and destroys the most human

[50] S. Dresden, *De literaire getuige*, Raster 57 Amsterdam 1986, 641-642.

characteristics in people. The fellow human being who stumbles is no longer given help but put away without compassion. No sensible person even suspects that people can fall so deeply. No one will understand it; no one will find the words to convey the macabre reality of it. Everything has been affected by death in advance.

From this time on Titus died continually: he let go of what he expected from this human existence, and abandoned himself to what became possible in the eyes of God. His deepest base was the certainty of his being beloved. "O Jesus, when I look on you My love for you becomes more true. And yours, I know, will never end: You see me as a special friend."

Kierkegaard once wrote that in every generation there are a few people who know and accept that it is their destiny to be sacrificed. In this religious certainty, which drives their executioners to madness, "they themselves are the ones who gives the command for their own execution." They are still unbroken people even at the moment of their demise. Precisely here, says Kierkegaard, lies the difference between a hero and a martyr: the hero offers resistance from within himself but the martyr receives his strength from God.

Raphael tells us how, along with Titus, he began the day. As always the story is disarming in its simplicity. Concealed behind his words, words he was able to record only years later, are strong – often exorbitant – feelings which he could calm down only after years of practice in simplicity and gentleness of living.

He tells us how the day began and what he did first thing in the morning. He helped Titus make up his bed. It brought home to him the supreme value of simple things. "Usually we do not talk about making up our bed." Raphael remembers, however, how when the first light of dawn shone through the windows of his barrack he bent down over Titus's bed and with his big hand smoothed out the gray blanket. He remembers with how much love and care he did this, it being practically the only thing he could do with love.

Titus, a physically exhausted man, stood by awkwardly, looking on and understanding it. After that they went out together for a brief meeting with the Polish brothers on Block 30. Father

Yanuszewski, the prior of the Carmelite monastery in Krakow who was beatified in 1981, and Albert Urbanski both spoke fluent German. The others did not understand Titus but were still eager to meet him because, as they said, Titus radiates such warmth. So they walked up and down the barrack a number of times.

After this brief encounter Titus and Raphael were by themselves again and quickly returned. As they went back Titus asked Raphael to pray the prayer of Our Lady of Mount Carmel. Titus could not remember the text. "Mary must help and assist us, dear brother," he said. "When she stretches out her hand over us, we can endure much."

Raphael relates these three items with which the day began in Dachau for both of them. It is a small triptych of short-lived moments in which the world was held together. In this strange world the insignificant things to which we usually pay no attention became highly significant. The will-to-live attached itself to them. Thus the men hid themselves in these small moments and were for a little while untouchable by the terror of the day.

Back in the barrack they hastily ate some bread and gulped down some coffee. Then they cleaned up their things, polishing some of them with newsprint. Then, having been chased out of the hall, they soon heard the command "antreten": stand ready for the general roll call.

> As we stood there, we were often struck by the splendid colors of the rising sun. The horizon then glowed with the most divergent shades of golden yellow and vermilion which then shaded into a deep purple and a glorious ultramarine. Often in the morning we all witnessed incredibly beautiful skies. No painter, I believe, has such colors on his palette to reproduce such miracles of nature with his brush. Such a sublime natural spectacle was then able, for a few moments, to focus your thoughts on him, the Creator of the universe, whose power and majesty knows no bounds.

"As long as such glittering spectacles of cloud-studded skies could take place in all colors, we *Häftlingen* (prisoners) could not be lost," writes Floris Bakels, who survived Dachau, in his book *Nacht und Nebel.* The diaries of concentration camp prisoners contain numerous expressions of the intense joy the prisoners felt when they experienced their freedom: the freedom to believe, to pray, to "undergo" the beauty of the sunrise and to enjoy nature but also, as Bakels writes, the bewildering contrast between "the beauty above and the ugliness here below."

In a letter dated June 18, 1943, and sent from the camp at Westerbork, Etty Hillesum wrote as follows as she watched people being loaded into freight cars:

> Not much heather is left within the barbed-wire fences: the number of barracks keeps growing. Only a small area is left in the far corner of the camp where I am now sitting, in the sun, under a splendid blue sky amidst the low shrubbery... Some 3,000 Jews are being shipped off again... The sky is full of birds; purple lupines grow here, standing in their princely, peaceful way. Two chatting old women have positioned themselves on the crate. The sun shines on my face and directly in front of our eyes mass murder is in progress: it is all so utterly incomprehensible.[51]

Such absurd scenes, as they become visible in the graphic descriptions of Raphael Tijhuis, are also a daily reality in Dachau. One given morning Raphael met Titus at the barrack. Titus was a bit hurried as he had forgotten his glasses. "But," says Raphael, "you cannot go in and get them now. It is *Stubendienst* (fatigue duty in the barracks). You are not allowed to go in." Raphael offered to sneak in himself for just a moment. Titus, firmly declining the offer, stepped into the hall, walking on tiptoe. The little door of his locker squeaked as he opened it. The senior officer on duty jumped and yelled: "Was ist los?" ("What's going on?") "Ich habe meine Brille vergessen, Herr Stubenälteste" ("I have forgotten my glasses, sir"). Titus tried to get away quickly but the senior officer, trained as a good Nazi, reacted promptly. "I will teach you to forget!" "A heavy blow with a club on Titus's head and his glasses fell in pieces on the ground. The man became furious, yelled, and hit Titus wherever he could. When, still uttering curses,

---

[51] Etty, De nagelaten geschriften van Etty Hillesum 1941-1943, Amsterdam 1986, 641-642.

the man went back to work, Titus scrambled to his feet, bleeding from his nose and mouth. Raphael picked up the pieces of his glasses. Anxiously he looked at Titus, wiping off the blood as well as he could. "Are you hurting badly?" he asked, finding it hard to suppress his fury against the Nazi officer. "Just be happy," said Titus, "that he did not beat you up like this."

In such a humiliating situation Titus probably thought of what Teresa of Avila wrote about the image of the suffering Christ that we have to bear within us and that we must intimately sympathize with. In 1927 Titus wrote: "Compared to this internal image, finally, that external image of wounds and stripes is something secondary; it is of value as the confirmation and deepening of that internal image."[52]

In his account of Titus's life and death in Dachau, Raphael Tijhuis repeatedly mentions the serenity and balance which Titus displayed there. Titus never lost it, even when he was kicked and beaten. There was no discernible sign in his behavior of hatred or aversion toward the Germans or the camp guards. He even still spoke with them in his own friendly way. By talking he still tried to achieve some kind of connection with them, but usually such conversation ended with a cuff around his ears or a kick.

> Afterward I sometimes said to Titus: "by all means, stop talking with those fellows. You will get nowhere with them; at best you'll get a thrashing." But then he would answer: "That is no reason to stop talking with them. Who knows what the effect will be? One must pray for these people," he frequently said, "so that they may gain some understanding." I have often seen Titus pray, and sometimes one had to remind him not to do this conspicuously, so that he would not be noticed by a member of the Block personnel and give him an excuse for administering a beating and for a volley of curses: "Come, let us go outside," he then said, "and together pray the rosary." Often we also prayed the morning prayer together and in that connection he would regularly ask me to pray that beautiful little prayer to Mary, since he himself no longer knew it completely by

[52] B. Borchert, Mystiek leven, een bloemlezing, Nijmegen 1985, 205.

heart. Every morning we thus walked up and down the Block street a few times, and if the "bear" then growled he often said: "now then: we had better start the new day in good spirits." And, laughing, he would then add: "In two months we will all be home again."

After the roll call the prisoners were always divided into Work Commandos. It was extremely important to get into a "light" Commando. That could mean, for example, a foreman who was less cruel; work that was done in the shade of a shed or a hall; work which involved getting an extra piece of bread or some soup. Such things could be a matter of survival.

Working in the herb garden

The rule for clergy was that they had no choices: "Pursuant to the communication dated 21-4-1942, German, Dutch, and Norwegian clergy must be put to work in the herb gardens in Dachau." This complex of herb gardens, the so-called "Plantation," was about 80 hectare in size and was located in a swampy area to the east of the camp. Every day some 1000 to 1200 prisoners were put to work there. Since working in the open field is very hard, the Plantation was a dreaded Commando. On the west side of the camp lay the "Liebhof" (Garden of Love). This farm, which was also called "Friedhof" (cemetery) on account of the many prisoners who died there, though not as large as the Plantation, demanded the same work. Aromatic herbs were grown there for their healing power. Everything that grew on the large fields there was directed toward life. The herbs alleviated pain and healed wounds. Working on these fields, however, was aimed at driving the clergy into death. Titus was put to work there early in July 1942. Raphael Tijhuis reports on a work day on the Liebhof as follows.

> As soon as a Titus was put to work outside the camp, on the Liebhof, he was allowed to exchange his wooden slippers for a pair of heavy shoes with wooden soles and rock-hard leather on top. Although this could sometimes mean a significant improvement, for Titus this trade was the primary reason why his feet were ruined with sores which, for lack of good nursing care, did not heal.

Initially it was just a matter of a few skin wounds, but soon these turned into large festering sores, the "Phlegmones," which gnawed away the flesh down to the bone and caused enormous pain.

I tore a towel into two sections which served well to bind Titus's wounds. Especially the putting on and taking off of the heavy shoes caused him much pain. Together we went outside and sat on the curb, for there was no opportunity inside. During the treatment Titus watched cautiously to make sure none of the Block personnel saw us. I then carefully took off his shoes, wiped the pus off his wounds with a piece of clean paper and then wrapped a piece of the towel around his foot. Granted, it took some effort to get his feet back into the shoes, but finally we succeeded again. I could see by his face that it had cost him a lot of pain but after I helped him get back on his feet, he would smile a little, pat me on the shoulder, and say: "There now, brother dear, I am the gentleman again."

To get to the Liebhof farm, Titus daily had to walk the road for almost three kilometers in the ill-fitting military shoes that were much too large for him, amidst the many marching, loudly-singing prisoners.

The primary job, especially during the summer months, was to weed, weed, and weed some more. All those crops like basil, savory, cumin, marjoram, thyme and whatever else their names might be, had to be regularly weeded, so that there were absolutely no weeds left in the beds. On close inspection this was not heavy work but the circumstances made it hard. In the first place, there were the long, long hours, under all sorts of weather conditions, either bent over or squatting down. In the summer time the scorching sun burned down on you, or in rainy weather one spent the whole day standing in the field in clothes that were soaking wet.

Other clergy as well have reported on the hard times they had on the Liebhof. Pastor Knoop tells his story:

In July 1942 we had a week of rain. All week long we had continued to work in the rain on the Liebhof and were soaked to the skin. Our clothes never got dry any more. Finally we could no longer do anything on the land except to ruin things, so that the camp leadership had to decide, when it was still raining on the sixth day of that

week, not to let us go out. The following morning it was still raining but we still marched out to work, but couldn't. The rain kept
pouring down in sheets. We stood in the middle of the large fields,
bent over, with our back to the wind, like cows in a pasture, while
the rain beat down on us without mercy.[53]

Toward noon the Liebhof Commando limped the three kilometers
back to the barrack for a paltry noon meal of watery soup and a
hunk of bread.

In the afternoon he came back to the Block dead-tired and was
happy as a child if someone brought him a carrot or piece of lettuce
from the field to "supplement" the skimpy noon meal. However
paltry and small our daily ration was, I still often witnessed how
Titus gave away a piece of it to a hungry fellow prisoner, saying:
"Here. Take it. You need it more than I do."

Not only were the prisoners given little food, the food they got
was bad. The eyes of the prisoners always wandered to look for
food: crusts of bread, carrots or beets if a person worked somewhere on the land; indeed, they looked for edible remnants even
in garbage cans. In this whole matter, however, Titus managed to
control himself exceptionally well. There is no doubt that he felt
the hunger as much as anyone else Not only the hard work he had
to do but also the malnutrition he suffered reduced his strength
very rapidly. He often said: "Who could ever have imagined that
we could dine so splendidly on a piece of bread and a couple of
'Pellmänner'?" ("Pellmänner": his word for the potatoes that had
been cooked in their jackets). "Let's be grateful to the good Lord,"
he would say. "Things could be worse."

When in the evening the order "abmarchieren" (march off!) had
been given, the dead-tired tormented prisoners dragged themselves
back to the camp. It frequently happened that Titus could almost
no longer stand or walk from sheer fatigue. In that case two
Polish Carmelites who also worked on the Liebhof would take him
between them and support him on the way back to the camp.

---

[53] J. Govers, *Stemmen uit Dachau*, Hapert 1990.

Alone, he could no longer cover that distance at the required marching pace.

Then when the prisoners, dead-tired, were back in the camp, it could sometimes take hours before the SS bothered to take the roll call. Raphael tells of the time when the guards somewhat relaxed their vigilance with respect to the height of the men [men of approximately the same height had to stand in the same line. Raphael was tall; Titus very short – Tr.] and he stood next to Titus at the evening roll call.

> There seemed to be no end to the waiting and we could only stay on our feet with difficulty. In passing I said to Titus: "How long do you suppose we have been standing here? What are we waiting for this time?" Laconically he replied: "My dear brother, let's have a little patience. We certainly have the time for it."

Titus remained totally serene. Raphael got angry: why the torture? Titus did not occupy himself with the question "why"? It remained senseless. "My dear brother: we have all the time in the world now." He made no attempt to assign any meaning to this torment. Nor did he utter a word of contempt. By this nimble-footed humor he elevated himself above the facts. It is typical of the mystic to be able to speak of the most obscure kinds of terror in a lighter vein. It is the mark of the spirit of disinterestedness.

The smile of an angel

The last three barracks on the main camp street on the left side, marked 26-28-30, were the preacher blocks which were usually called the "priest-barracks." Approximately 2,600 clergymen lived here. Striking was the great diversity in religions, as well as age and ranks. Here, however, all these differences had ceased to matter: everyone wore the same clothing, was given a balding shave, and got the same meager food. This large community was composed of 24 different nationalities and 39 different orders and congregations were represented in it. Catholic clergy had the advantage of being able to talk to each other *in Latin*.

In March 1941 the priest barracks were surrounded by a special barbed-wire fence and thus formed a camp of their own as it were in the concentration camp. The Germans were extremely fearful of the influence of the faith and of the authority of spiritual leaders. The priests, given the chance, came together to celebrate the Eucharist. They did this in the field or in some concealed corner of the dormitory or secretly in a loft. They collected grains of wheat and baked the wafers for the celebration themselves. A few of them, distributed over a wide arc, kept a lookout.

One morning the priests of Block 26 who were weeding the herb garden to their great astonishment saw a girl of about ten walking shyly toward them. Imagine: a child who knew only the innocent freedom of her little world, hesitantly stepping forward in the direction of the forced laborers who were deeply bent over their work. With wonderment in her eyes she looked at the tired gray faces of the men. A couple of men raised themselves up and gave her a searching look. She then dropped a small canister in an open space between the plants. In a reverently whispering voice she said; "Da ist der liebe Herr Gott drinnen" ("Our dear Lord God is inside"). The men understood. One of them took the canister and carefully hid it in his clothing. It was the day of Corpus Christi. Their minds turned to the solemn celebration and the sacramental procession everywhere in the free world. Someone must have sent the little girl. The man behind this action was the priest of the Jacob parish in the little town of Dachau: prelate Pfanzell. He found out where the priests had to perform their forced labor. The idea occurred to him to involve this little girl, a daughter of a family he knew, in an action he had planned. A touching thought! The little girl was told to go to the plantation and ask if she could buy a bouquet of gladioli. She was given a canister of communion wafers and had to see to it that it got into the hands of the priests without being noticed.

From that time on the little girl came at regular times to buy her gladioli. Before long they called her "the little angel of Dachau." When she returned home on her little bike, one of the priests would go to the place where the canister with the wafers lay.

He fingered it with reverence. To him it was the Bread of Life. It lay on the moist earth of this field of exhaustion and death. It lay amidst medicinal herbs which were not intended for the forced laborers. For them there was no longer anything to hold onto in the visible and verifiable world. They knew that they increasingly had to relax their grip on that world.

The priests now received Holy Communion very differently from the way they were used to. They experienced it entirely anew as an unknown source of strength. The Bread of Life which they ate together in the shadow of death gave them the strength to break with all confidence in the external world, the walls and ramparts with which we surround ourselves, and to enter into the free space within. This little field of the soul would never be entirely pure. Traces of overly strong self-seeking will always remain. These traces can be found in the inclination to ensconce ourselves behind trifles, tiny attachments, but also in the urge primarily to secure our own existence even at the expense of fellow human beings. The mystery of evil will be part of this existence to the hour of the harvest. This reality no longer unhinged them. The confidence that they were the good seed of the field increased. They would fall into the dark bosom of the earth. Many of them would die here and open up in newness of life, of union with him whom they had sought their whole life.

In Block 26, where the German clergy lived a primitive chapel had been arranged since January 1941, where the Eucharist could be celebrated every morning. This, however, applied only to German priests. All others were excluded from it. But in barrack 28 the men knew this. Here, too, the wafers were handed on in hidden ways. Many people received Holy Communion in secret. Thus the Capuchin pater Othmarus Lips relates that he and other prisoners a few times received the holy host from Titus Brandsma. Raphael remembers how Titus too knew himself strengthened by the realization that Christ was with him. One evening he gave a holy host to Titus who, Raphael tells us, kept it inside the hem under the belt of his pants. After the evening roll call the prisoners washed their feet and then all looked for their bed, longing for rest. On their way to bed the prisoners had to pass by the *Stubenäl-teste* to be checked. The latter searched their clothing to ensure they did not even have a strip of material with them with which to bind their wounds. When Raphael entered the sleeping quarters he saw that Titus's bed was still empty. Suddenly he heard the roaring voice of the *Stubenälteste:* "Ha, Brandsma, you swineherd." Frightened, Raphael looked around and saw Titus standing before the man. Titus and a number of other men had apparently failed to clean their feet properly. Raphael kept anxiously looking on from the sleeping quarters. Again the man began to yell. "I will teach you how to keep clean!" He kept repeating this, screaming loudly. At the same time he began to deliver blows. Raphael shuddered with fear. Titus had wrapped the host in the white piece of paper it came with and hidden it in his glasses case, which he had kept with him in his armpit. The man approached Titus and raised his club, screaming "Auch Du bist so ein Drecksack" ("You, too, are a filthy bastard"). The club came down hard, and Titus tumbled to the ground. This really aroused the man's fury. He beat and kicked Titus wherever he could. Titus, rolling over and crawling, tried to reach the threshold of the sleeping quarters. The man, meanwhile, kept beating and kicking him, all the while screaming. Finally Titus succeeded in dragging his sore body over the threshold. The moment Raphael saw this, he ran to Titus and lifted him up wrapping his arms around him and bringing him to his bed. Covering Titus warmly with his big hands, he asked if he hurt a lot. Now if Titus should say that he did, Raphael would of course caress his painful limbs all the more compassionately. But Titus was thinking of a very different form of consolation. He looked at Raphael with a smile and whispered: "My dear brother, remember I knew whom I was carrying with me." At the same time he pointed to his glasses case which he cautiously kept hidden under his left arm.

Raphael became very quiet. Suddenly a rush of holy reverence came over him. Titus, seeing this, said: "Come, let us pray an *Adoro Te*." Raphael wanted to sink down on his knees, but Titus softly cautioned: "Be careful. They must not see us pray." In a whisper they prayed to the God who was with him: "With great reverence I pray to you, O hidden God." Then Titus gave the benediction with the Holy of Holies in the glasses case. "And now quickly off to bed," he said in conclusion.

There is in this story a precious moment when Titus, responding to Raphael's anxious question whether he was hurting a lot, whispered "My dear brother, remember I knew whom I was carrying with me." Titus's smile and the screaming of the Nazi officer: the contrast between the spiritual man and the physical man. The time of screaming is usually short. The time of physical violence does not last long. We cannot live with it.

The smile of the angel in the cathedral at Reims is the answer to the demonic figures so abundantly present in the Roman style. The smile overcomes the anxiety of the terrifying, the monstrous. The Nazi officer with the bull's neck screamed; he always screamed. He drove people apart and beat them down. He sowed fear and panic all around him and was soon satisfied. He never had emotions which penetrated deeply into the core of his being, which were permanent, and could change him.

Titus's smile was liberating. It was the smile of a purified person. He had found himself back. In other words: he received himself anew with a trust that was altogether pure. His smile in the barrack of Dachau and his tears in the cell at Kleve came from the same source: "Now I know again that You love me."

Raphael was quiet and profoundly moved. For almost three years more he retained this image of the terror of the camp and after that for the rest of his life. The following morning Raphael asked Titus whether he had had a good night's sleep. "After two o'clock I could not sleep anymore, but from that time on I spent the night in prayerful adoration."

Titus took the night as it came, not experiencing it, so dark and full of pain, as a defeated person who powerlessly waits for the dawn to break. He accepted the unavoidable and gave to it a significance of its own. In his earlier days, in the church of the monastery, a night-long worship service was held a few times every year. The Holy of Holies stood on the altar between burning candles and flowers. Small groups of people relieved each other to pray for some time in silence. These were the quiet hours of worship Titus had in mind. Instead of the monstrance and the festive flowers there was the glasses case in which the holy host was kept securely hidden. He filled the lonely, empty night with a wealth of meaning. The "unavoidable" was the material with which he worked, like a sculptor chipping away at a piece of marble and giving it a face. This arose from an inalienable inner freedom. In all quietness he told Raphael how the night had been. There was no sign of the forced nature of anxious self-assertion. Titus was utterly concentrated on God as the One who was present and near. He was not destroyed by suffering. The man who beat and kicked him could kick him when he lay doubled up on the ground but he could not touch his interior life. Titus remained himself, the man he had always been, preserved his composure, and remained unshaken in his confidence that good is stronger than evil.

Suffering people often manifest an unprecedented intensity of life, something we learn again from the testimonies of death camp survivors. It is well that this should not be forgotten. It is a remarkable – sometimes unsuspected – aspect of suffering. Also in everyday life we encounter simple people who in their suffering mature into authentic personalities. There is in them a palpable strength which transcends them. These experiences can give us a deeper insight into the essential nature of humanity. It makes us ask what the real sources are from which people draw their greatest strengths. Titus was no longer "anybody." But there was the contrasting reality of his inner strength. The humiliations he suffered did not make him an embittered man.

The Capuchin pater Othmarus comments: "An eternal smile full of patience and inner serenity, a smile of mystical resignation in all the suffering he had to bear, marked Titus. He had been maltreated so badly that his teeth literally hung loose in his mouth. He repaid all that with the prayer of Christ: 'Father, forgive them.' Neither I nor anyone else ever heard him complain. He was a saint."

The Feast of Our Lady of Mount Carmel

It was July 16, the solemn memorial celebration of our Lady of Mount Carmel. A few men, all of them dressed in ill-fitting prison clothing, had looked each other up and were inconspicuously assembled on the shady side of a gray barrack. Gathered there were Titus Brandsma, Raphael Tijhuis, Bruno Makowski, Albert Urbanski, Hilary Yanuszewski, the prior of Mount Carmel of Krakow, and a few other Carmelites. A secular priest from Poland had joined them. Even before his arrest he had indicated his desire to become a member of the Third Order of the Carmelites. He was in the process of preparing himself for membership. By the simple gesture of the laying on of hands Titus admitted him to the fellowship of the order.

At that moment the special life of Mount Carmel was closer to them than everything they saw around them. They had come from different countries and probably never met each other before. But drawing their inspiration from the same spiritual tradition, they clearly recognized each other. This gave them a sense of connectedness which was very familiar to them. They experienced this as a timeless moment which briefly lifted them above the terrors of the moment. With heads shaven bald and their emaciated hands they stood in a circle before the face of God, whose will is above all. Knowing that thus alone they could unmask their fate, they experienced the mystery of existence in a new, enlightened manner.

Together, amidst hatred and despair, clacking boots and false slogans, in an atmosphere filled with the odor of death and the fear of dying far from home, they celebrated the Feast of Mount Carmel. Thus they joined hands in order, in defiance of the horrible situation in which they found themselves, to remember with joy that here, too, they could live and persevere under the protection of Mary. They knew themselves connected with the Carmel experience elsewhere in the world. Perhaps, as is the custom among Carmelites, they concluded their get-together by praying the *Salve Regina* together: "gementes et flentes in hac lacrimarum valle" ("sighing and weeping in this valley of tears").

In the shadow of death

On the herb fields of the Liebhof Titus felt his last powers ebb
away. He had worked for many hours – bent over forward in the
mud. It had already rained for days. His Calvary had become too
heavy for him. The end – dark but definite – was approaching.
One can no longer say what he experienced or felt. He was like a
stranger who found himself in a world where he was not supposed
to be. He almost palpably experienced that everything – this whole
misshapen world – is a grand illusion. All this, right down to his
outsized prison smock which hung around his thin shoulders,
including his wounded and emaciated body, was unreal. But his
mind – only his mind – kept his original self intact. His inner core
preserved its original strength. Everything around him was full of
darkness and deception: the world as it was not meant to be.

In a boundless moment of light Titus Brandsma saw the other
world. There human beings find the right resonance; there they see
the radiance of a higher order, as in "The Walled-in Garden" with
its fragrant plants and flowers: the garden of true life. The gate is
wide open…. A few caring arms of fellow prisoners bent down
over Titus and lifted him up from the moist earth. He wrapped his
bony arms around their shoulders. He stumbled and awakened in
the real world of camp life. For a moment he had seen the truth,
but it was gone again. "A little while," he sighed, "and we shall be
free again."

Titus Brandsma ended up in a world he did not know. He did
not try to understand this. He had gotten to the point where nothing of the evil surrounding him could be understood any more. He
had been surrounded on all sides by evil, locked up in it as in a
cell. But the walls of the cell could not bury him. From that location he remained hopeful to the end. This was based on his vital
spirit but even more on his belief that we are not delivered up to
our fate but that God sustains our life.

Titus preserved his inner serenity when he was beaten. He consistently looked for the real powers in his inner life. He saw
the implausibility of the falsification of the world around him.

This world focuses on an externalization which is foreign to the essence of humanity. The Lord of the field with the good seed and the weeds has the final say. Titus knew this. When the reality around him unraveled and fell apart in meaninglessness, this truth remained sharply engraved in his mind. Evil remains mysterious in its violent course and stealthy ways. So much has remained hidden, so much has been forgotten, there was so much deceit, so much had been misjudged by people – but one day the true verdict will be pronounced.

It was July 18. Three men stumbled with difficulty down the muddy country road which led back from the herb field to the camp. They were two Polish Carmelites, Hilary Yanuszewski and Albert Urbanski, with Titus Brandsma between them. He had wrapped his arms around their shoulders. When he released his grip for just a moment, he tottered. He was totally exhausted. It was his last journey.

Evening was approaching. A dark evening glow descended over the fields. They were underway to the final stopping place, where insanity and degeneracy reached its nadir. Denied all human consolation, they dragged themselves painfully to this inhospitable resort. On this final journey Titus perhaps thought for a brief moment of his attempt, not long ago, to escape this horror. But God's ways are always different from our calculations. An unprecedented serenity crept into his tortured soul. Now that everything fell away, he knew "there is no salvation other than by Your grace." He accepted that. From that time on a new peace entered his tormented soul.

Titus became aware that the ancient pledge made at the time of his entry into the order would now be fulfilled for the last time. In a sober ritual the new arrival received the habit of the Carmelites. After that the brothers of the monastic community received him, singing, in their midst. They wished him happiness as they sang and repeated the line: "Ecce quam bonum et quam jucundum habitare fratres in unum" ("Behold, how good it is, and how pleasant, where brothers are together, dwelling in unity"). It is a brotherhood in which self-interest increasingly recedes into the background and the uniqueness of each member is valued. Brotherhood is more than the sum of individuals. Brotherhood confers a new quality of life which begins to grow from the moment one becomes conscious of it. Many view the rest and constancy which they experience in this unity as a great blessing in their life. By comparison with brotherly community, love has more vehemence and fire. The Carmelites in the death camps experienced the durability and constant warmth of brotherly life as a very special quality which was never lost. In the sparse moments in which they met each other – inconspicuously in safe places – they experienced brotherhood as never before. This brotherly affection, purified and ennobled into mystical attention, was the last benefit Titus received in Dachau. Now the final journey of all his wanderings had ended.

Back in the barrack Raphael Tijhuis was present when Titus allowed himself to be persuaded by his fellow brothers to be admitted in the infirmary.

> In the sick barrack I said good-bye to pater Titus who thanked me for all the help he had received. He then passed along still more greetings for the rest of the men on our block. "It is only for a few days," he said. "For the rest, my dear brother, come August we'll all be home again," he added with laughter. These were the last words I heard from his mouth. We never saw him again.

A few times Titus saw at his sickbed his Polish fellow brother Yanuszewski who had been admitted sick in the same barrack. For Titus this was certainly a source of much consolation. When Titus was totally exhausted, when he suffered down to the core of his soul and prayed for mercy, he knew that every word was heard. There is a God whom nothing escapes. There is a force greater than all other forces, a force which works creatively and healingly, and which is recognized as pure love. Titus became conscious that this God of love again called him to come out of himself. He felt that from the depths of space a force arose by which he could again raise himself up. But this belongs to a part of his most intimate life story. His confidence in God's loving care and his attempt to find concrete ways to let this loving care penetrate his daily life were a vital element in the history of his life.

It was Sunday, July 26, 1942, two o'clock in the afternoon. The nurse passed along to the office the news that no. 30492 had died. The next day his body was cremated.

Like a light, he went out in the darkness of exhaustion and abandonment. Many are astonished that this light preserved its power and incandescence unhindered.

In the Beginning the End is Can Be Seen

It was a strange world in which Titus ended up after his arrest. The capriciousness of evil took on bizarre forms. The machinery from which the events originated and found their way was dark and incomprehensible.

At the same time a familiar rhythm emerged in the succession of events, a rhythm that could not remain hidden. In Scheveningen he was in a cell. For Titus it was a place of inwardness, of silence, and lonely dedication. In Amersfoort he was in a barrack. There he was among people, oriented to others, dedicated to others. Many become immersed in their social passions and in the process turn away from God, or conversely: they devote themselves to God, science, or a solitary career as a poet and turn away from society. Titus, by contrast, experienced these two sides of life as a spontaneously merging unity. Later there was again the solitariness of the cell in Kleve and being together with many in the barracks in Dachau. This is the rhythm of introversion and extraversion, of closing up and of giving oneself like a flower.

These periods seem to succeed each other like a repetition. But the return to the cell and then again to the barracks is not merely a repetition. In Scheveningen and Amersfoort he lived and spoke from the riches of his knowledge and experience, as that became evident from his interrogation, his defense, his speech about Geert Grote. In Kleve and Dachau he realized that he had been abandoned by the authorities. This realization shocked him deeply. After a severe inner conflict he surrendered. He no longer expected a rescue. The only thing that was strongly alive in him was the realization that he was in God's hands and that his dignity was inviolable. In Scheveningen, after all, he had written: "I know that You love me."

For that reason he could also continue to see the dignity of his fellow human beings, even in spite of the evil to which these fellow men gave themselves up. The last thing in his life was to be among people, to open himself up to them, to give what he still had to give. This respect for humans was deeply rooted in his very being. This respect, accordingly, was always spontaneous and unintentional. Precisely because his desire to give something to people for their life's journey came from his inner disposition, this component always came as an inspiration: without calculation, at just the right moment.

The last person to whom he gave of himself was the nurse who, together with the camp physician, visited him in the sick barrack. In an interrogation on May 38, 1956, she testified about the final days and death of Titus Brandsma. She felt a need to talk, "to render a service to pater Titus Brandsma, since I have a lot to make up for, and out of gratitude: he helped me a lot."

During one week she visited him twice daily. She relates that the death of Titus was a certainty. The Germans, after all, fostered a strong hatred against highly placed priests. The physician designated Titus as one who should be given the "finishing injection." Titia, as she is called in the official record, says that he felt very sorry for her.

> Titus asked me what led me to work here. One day he took my hand and said: "What a poor girl you are. I pray for you a lot." He told me about his monastery in Nijmegen. Once he asked me to take along a letter and to mail it secretly. I accepted the letter but later I tore it up. He also gave me his rosary but I told him I could not pray. Then he said: "At least pray the last words: pray for us sinners." Then I had to laugh.
>
> Whenever you came into the infirmary there was a group of sick people, all stooped and bent by fatigue and pain, standing around Titus's bed. With a lonely death facing them they looked for a last

moment of comfort in each other's company. They found it especially by Titus's bedside. There was in him something that gave
people confidence.

We know that Titia was present when a man, standing close to his
bed, told him in tears about his life. She heard Titus say: "but my
good man, certainly that is not so bad; that is all in the past."
According to her, Titus's attitude was striking because most sick
prisoners were only occupied with themselves, but Titus was always
in a good mood.

In her report the nurse says that people sought him out for his
calm and friendliness. The source from which his strength came
was deeper. Titus lived on the strength of his conviction that
humans are not abandoned to themselves, that they belong to God,
and that God's power works in them. The deepest level of a human
life is only fulfilled in that relation to God.

This does not mean that he sealed himself off from the world
outside of him and spun a cocoon for himself in a protected interior world of his own. He remained an open and receptive person
but did not let himself be overpowered by the superior power of
evil. He saw the relativity, the transient character, of violence. This
world could not penetrate the core of his being where he kept the
holy experience of God's inviolable nearness. Accordingly, he did
not ask himself: Why does especially this misfortune happen to
me? He took the days as they came. Behind everything he assumed
the existence of an order which he respected.

The characteristic trait of his life became more clearly evident
toward the end. In these last days the splendor of his humility came
out. That is the attitude of the person who realizes that he does not
have his life in his own hands but who accepts it and everything
that happens in it as coming from God. This humility does not
mean anything without a strong will to live. It takes a lot of
courage, after all, to accept even the most dreadful parts of one's
life.

In his thinking a light had entered which filled him with a different wisdom. In his actions he experienced a power which led

him to that which, left to his own devices, could only fill him with fear. This can only be understood in the light of his humility. It takes real courage to consent to it without raising objections.

The sick around his bed recognized the total serenity of his heart. They tried to hold onto the consolation of the moment. Nor did it escape the nurse. She preserved the memory which changed her life.

His powers rapidly diminished. After two days the physician prepared an injection. That was according to plan. From the beginning, after all, his name occurred on the death list.

> After that I personally administered the injection in his right wrist. It was ten minutes to two and at two o'clock he died. It was July 26, 1942. At that point the physician and I left the room. After that, according to the prevailing custom, the staff undressed the body and threw it into a pit. Then they scattered quicklime over it. Sometimes they also poured gasoline over it which they then ignited. I do not know what they did with Titus's body.

Dictators who stop at nothing to torture and to kill in their passion to destroy people go so far that they even wish to wipe out the memory of the existence of their victims. To them the people in the camps have no name: they are simply a number. The smoking chimneys of the incinerators and the stacks of bodies thrown away in the deep pits are the last signs of that existence.

The victims are now among us anew in monuments of stone or marble, materials by which they are clothed with a new dignity. The nameless people have now become martyrs, heroes of the resistance, or saints. Thus their names will continue to live among us. Thus, too, the memory of their suffering will take on a permanent form. That memory encompasses the suffering of all times and will as a vital force purify human life and awaken our deeper forces in the times that lie ahead.

PRINTED ON PERMANENT PAPER • IMPRIME SUR PAPIER PERMANENT • GEDRUKT OP DUURZAAM PAPIER - ISO 9706

N.V. PEETERS S.A., KLEIN DALENSTRAAT 42, B-3020 HERENT